Daydreams:
A book of sonnets

Jim "Buddy" Ivey 1942–1992 (c. 1962)

Daydreams:
A book of sonnets

The Collected Works
of
James R. Ivey, Sr.

Compiled and Edited
By
James R. Ivey (Jr.)

Ivey Leaf Publishing
Albuquerque, New Mexico

An Ivey Leaf Publishing Publication
All rights reserved

Copyright 2017

Published and distributed in the United States by:

Ivey Leaf Publishing
Albuquerque, NM 87122

Editors: James R. Ivey, Jr. / Alysa Ivey
Cover/Interior Design: Ted Roach
Design Consultant: Stacie Ivey
Cover Photo: Peshkov/Adobe Stock
Author Photo (Ivey, Jr): Charles Lebeau

For comments, stories, or additional information contact jivey1215@yahoo.com or iveyleafpublishing@gmail.com.

Published 2017, second printing 2018
Printed in the United States of America

Ivey, James R.
Daydreams: A book of sonnets
SBN-13: 978-0998180199
ISBN-10: 099818019X
BISAC: Poetry: American, General

DEDICATION

To Theresa Rose Ivey - Guidry

the Louisiana Lady...

"To you, who are as saintly as your name,
Herewith, I dedicate this heart and verse;
Each hour with you shines like a gift from God,
Radiating love's sweet light into my life.
Earth is graced by your ways of perfection,
Sacred to me is your purest love;
And so, I give you this glimpse of my soul,
Theresa. God, I thank you, for my wife."

~James R. Ivey, Sr.
(married May 10, 1964)

James R. Ivey

TABLE OF CONTENTS

James R. Ivey

James R. Ivey

A Note to the Reader

"Every man's life ends the same way. It is only in the details of how he lived and how he died that distinguish one man from another."
~*Ernest Hemingway*

Daydreams is a collection of poetry over 65 years in the making. My father wrote and won an award for his first poem in 1950 when he was 8-years-old, and crafted over 200 poems across the next 42 years. His tenacity and love for writing poetry amazed me.

My dad, the "Alabama Dinosaur," was born and raised in Dothan, Alabama. When he wasn't writing poetry, he was selling cars. I recall the recurring scene from my childhood: him working with diligence at his desk, papers scattered all about, and me always attempting to drag him away to play catch or go fishing. Half of the time I was successful; when I wasn't, I would get his standard story of how he was struggling with 'the reluctant muse.' I was aware of how difficult the writing process was, as well as how much happier he was and how his world made more sense when he was immersed in his art.

One of the lessons he imparted to my older sisters (Nikki and Tracy) and me was how important it is to cultivate your imagination. My sisters and I grew up as children of modest means, with few opportunities for travel, but my dad would always say how that shouldn't limit us. "How can you possibly be bored, when you have the gift of daydreaming?" he would often ask, going on about how "we use the same parts of our brain to imagine doing something as actually doing it." Then he would insist, "Use your imagination and go travel to distant lands!" and off I would go to explore the world. Today I am grateful he shared his love of daydreaming with us. I believe it was through the act of daydreaming that his creativity flowed.

My father and I began to collaborate on editing and arranging his poetry when I started college in 1988. I knew he had spent many years

writing poetry, but I was taken aback by how prolific he was in producing hundreds of poems. It was through our joint project that I came to know my dad on a deeper level. Unfortunately, our collaboration on the project was never completed due to my father's untimely death in 1992 at only 50 years of age.

During those last days of his terminal illness, I promised him I would complete our project and get his poems published. I regret to say life got in the way, and all his handwritten poems and notes were stowed away on shelves. Through the years, I have resumed and paused numerous times, derailed by life's circumstances. As we now approach the 25th anniversary of his passing, I am excited to finally relay his life's work and creative spirit to the world. Long overdue, it is my hope that you enjoy this window into his mind and that, like me, it stimulates daydreams within you.

The Writing Style

"Two roads diverged in a wood, and I –
I took the one less traveled by,
And that has made all the difference."
~Robert Frost

My father was a true "Sonneteer" born five centuries late. His favorite form of poetry to compose was the sonnet. The sonnet originated with Italian poet Giacomo Da Lentini in the early 13th century. The form is a lyric poem consisting of 14 lines, following a specific structure and strict rhyme scheme. A sonnet expresses different aspects of a single thought, mood, or feeling. It is resolved or summarized in the last lines of the poem. Sonnets were originally accompanied by mandolin or lute music.

Dad's favorite form of sonnet was the English or Shakespearean style. This style, though less rich in rhyme than the Italian style (a note from his journal), consists of three quatrains each rhymed differently. Culminating in a final, independently rhymed couplet that incites an effective, unifying climax or unexpected turn to the whole.

The collected work of poems, *Daydreams*, is comprised of seven distinct books, each covering a different theme. Each book consists largely of Shakespearian sonnets, a few Petrarchan (Italian style) sonnets, and experimental poems of other forms at the end of each book.

James R. Ivey

Book 1

The Reluctant Muse

James R. Ivey

Alone at Sea

I find myself alone at sea.

I search the distance for some land

That waits with freedom for a man;

There's just forever here...and me.

My sailing here has been life's chore

My journey one of real emotion

A man in transit on life's ocean

Until, again, I've come to shore.

The natives here survey my boat.

Better men, they say, survived those waves;

For proof, they point at unmarked graves,

And seem surprised my craft would float.

Again, I am alone at sea

There's just forever here...and me.

Anachronism

Lord, if I can only have more time

To practice this most ancient art;

I'll re-dedicate my soul and heart

To perfect my meter, mind, and rhyme.

When I was born, I had no choice

It was ordained that I write verse;

I thought my fate could not be worse,

And saw no reason to rejoice...

But now, at last, I realize

You had some work for me to do;

And this talent was a tool from you

To build a man who could be wise.

Was I born three centuries late...

Or put here now for something great?

Art and Craft

I have put my soul into my art!

But my muse still asks much more from me,

And from my craft I call 'Poetry'...

She doubts the courage within my heart.

Does a lifetime sailed on land-locked lakes

And rivers of shallow emotion

Prepare a bard to brave the ocean?

I'm best at tea and parlor cakes!

What happens when I lose sight of shore?

Can I learn, at sea, to navigate?

I would hate to be known as 'The Late.'

She says real art requires I risk more!

"But what if, dear muse, my craft goes down?"

"You'll learn to swim...or you'll learn to drown."

Birds, Words, and Trees

My thoughts fly free like birds,

And I don't know the words

To lure them to this cage

And pin them to this page.

This page was once a tree,

A living thing like me;

It loved the kiss of rain

Then learned the world's insane.

Does it remember words

Learned from nesting birds?

If it owns a memory

Why should it share with me?

Are there nightmares of attacks

By axed-up lumberjacks?

Butterflies

Butterflies are fleeing flowers

Who will not serve their few short hours

Chained to a rock-filled garden space,

Or jailed within life's prison vase.

They will not serve, or stand and wait,

To be still victims of chance or fate;

They move because they do not care

To decorate our ladies' hair.

Watching them make those frantic starts

Is pleasing to my eyes and heart;

Who does not feel some sharp regret

To see them caught in life's cruel net?

I believe it is the poet's duty

To aid and abet such magic beauty.

Comma

We often pause, here in the south,

With our pencils, and with our mouth;

We try to keep, our brains in gear,

So, what we think, is what you hear.

English poets, have longer breath;

Pentameter, scares me to death!

That many words, will make me stall...

Southern poets, have southern drawls.

There are those, that as we speak,

Are branding me, a comma freak!

Why should the presence, of a comma,

Cause some critics, mental trauma?

Some say I'm in, a comma coma;

The world is holding, my diploma.

Computer Operator

All lovely ladies give me pleasure,

They bring me joy beyond all measure;

I consider each a private treasure,

And their memories belong to me.

I file them on discs within my mind,

And pull them up when I have the time;

An idle hour can become sublime

Programming beauty into memory.

Angelic charm and sensuous grace,

The perfect form, the fabulous face;

All safely entered and stored in place,

Awaiting recall commands from me.

IBM should not feel so clever...

Poets have used computers forever.

Dark Lady

I guess that I need to run an ad.

My only lover is my sweet wife,

There is no turmoil in my slow life.

"Dark lady needed. She must be bad!"

I need the lady to break my heart,

And fill me with creative power

To write a sonnet every hour,

I need her now to quicken my art.

She'll bring me passion and great despair,

And she'll be generous with my friends.

Hey! It worked before. Why not again?

I'll write fast sonnets to her dark hair!

My wife just voted and she said no...

She prefers sonnets be written slow.

Daydreaming

There are places where I can go,

And leave the pressures of today;

Places where I can get away,

And be someone my friends don't know.

Are these journeys just fantasy?

When I leave there and come back home

I know much more of Greece and Rome,

And all I learn comes home with me.

I've made love to Helen in Troy,

And Cleopatra on the Nile;

Both ask me please to stay awhile,

But I don't daydream just for joy.

Today, I studied with Petrarch...

(Laura wants me when it gets dark!)

Daydreams

Some Austrian poet should have warned Freud,

Daydreams are normal and great tools of art;

They're fountains of truth that flow from the heart,

And not mental illness man should avoid.

Psychologists now are getting clever,

They've discovered daydreams keep us healthy,

And have, throughout history, made men wealthy.

They're learning new things we've known forever.

By mixing daydreams with reality

Wise men have gleaned from within themselves

Those golden volumes on library shelves,

And the philosophies that keep men free.

Daydreams work as wishing wells for pleasure,

Perfect places for thoughts that we treasure.

Epitaph for a Poet

All men must die, but you must never weep,

When you recall my frail body is gone;

Man walks until tired, then body must sleep,

But the soaring soul of the poet lives on.

Remember me often, but not with a tear,

Let the light from a smile play on your face:

Say he was a good man with conscience clear,

Who has gone to, and left, a better place.

Say cold clouds of dark Death can never shroud

Nor chill my fiery dreams I burned in rhyme;

Death claimed the body, but my spirit unbowed

Lives in my verse, and is locked in her prime.

Say Death was duped by duality,

My soul soars free of mortality!

Fame

The seeds I've sown grow through life's soil,

And now it's time to harvest and toil;

To harvest, for better or worse,

The planted prose and potted verse.

Once fall seemed fifty years away,

Now spring, it seems, was yesterday;

One season is too short a span

To take full measure of a man.

The young planter and I are one,

Who wondered West just like the sun;

We both are now in afternoon

And know sunset is coming soon.

Will I harvest the fame I crave,

Or lie nameless in shallow grave?

Fishing and Fighting

Poems are swimming in the air...

To catch us some I need a net;

I haven't hooked that big one yet...

She will not fish...my muse don't care.

Fragments are floating everywhere...

I think some parts could make some whole,

And put some romance in our soul...

My muse wears curlers in her hair.

I have not started any fires...

She does not tremble at my touch;

I guess I don't impress her much...

I'm not the lover she desires.

When I take her by force, it seems,

Byron and Keats dance in her dreams.

Fleeting Fame

When I was eight, I won a prize for verse.

Suddenly, I was a real somebody,

And became a major celebrity.

They put my picture right in the paper!

My poem was displayed in the window

Of the downtown Dothan Book and Art Store.

I'd go and stand around when school let out,

And watch big people stop and look at it.

I expected a call from Hollywood,

Or at least a contract from Bennet Cerf.

My sister thought I must be Jesus Christ!

After a week, they took my poem out.

Before long, I was nobody again,

And my sister punched me in the stomach.

For Me, it is!

I once thought fame would be mine soon

The world would celebrate my art,

And recognize my noble heart...

Time stole the air from that balloon!

With magic in my heart and hand

I write sweet songs to sing out loud,

But find no favor with the crowd...

My talent's not in much demand.

I have no money now at all.

No curtain calls or critics praise

Will interrupt my final days...

I should have studied basketball!

For those few fans who think I'm great:

Go bounce a ball! It ain't too late!

Free Verse

Poverty has never been funny...

Today, it seems, that my verse is 'free',

For there's no money, in poetry...

And there's no poetry, in money!

As a victim of this bardic curse,

I'm a captive here caught out of time,

And sentenced to sing my unheard rhymes

To a world that loves to hate true verse.

Can fortune, or fame, still lie ahead?

When the world was young she loved this art,

And held her poets close to her heart...

When the world finds me, will I be dead?

Packed in new cartons that cannot last,

We're still the products of our own past.

Genesis

All poets are created equal.

That's our story. There is no sequel.

Twenty-six letters! That's our lot.

That's what we have. That's all we got.

At least, with English, that is so.

With Japanese? I will not know!

I studied Latin in my youth.

Forgot it all...and that's the truth!

Should I be more continental?

Would that cure my problems dental?

If I became more debonair,

Could I re-grow my missing hair?

I think I'll stay. I'll take the chance,

That I can make these fellows dance.

James R. Ivey

How Many Marks Make a Dollar?

All my marks for fame float on life's waters.

That makes it hard to total up your score.

Maybe nothing I do will ever count.

Today, I made many new water marks:

I played tag football with my little son,

And wrote a sonnet that my dog adored;

My daughter gave me a pretty flower,

A smile, and a sweet grimy garden kiss;

I found a strange old book I had forgot,

And saw my reflection in a woman's eyes.

Things are bound to be better for us soon.

Maybe today a newspaper ad will

Ask to hire an unknown Southern poet.

Or the Winter might freeze my floating marks.

The Hunter

I stalked a rare idea within my brain.

I sensed, much more than saw, my wary prey;

At my approach, like smoke, it shied away,

And all my searching effort was in vain.

The darkness of my mind was its domain,

It seemed some fear of light kept it at bay;

The weary weeks piled up, until one day

I cried: "In dumb darkness you shall remain!"

But then, it seemed to turn and follow me.

Less wary now that I should sense a sound

In dimness, near to sleep, with light to see

The hunter by, the trophy then was found.

Tired of wild freedom, and too tired to flee,

It came and slept beside me on the ground.

I Must

People ask me: "Why do you write?"

It's just a thing that I must do

Like breathing is a thing for you;

Why does daylight struggle with night?

Order from chaos! That's my goal.

As darkness moves within my mind

I work to see where I am blind...

I must attempt to take control.

I've stored my talent on life's shelf.

Sometimes, for years, I left my art

Without the rhythm of my heart,

And was a stranger to myself.

Perhaps, in truth, I don't know why...

A man must live...or he must die.

Job Application

My college grades were mostly A's,

Tests say I have a high I.Q.;

There must be something I can do

To land a job that really pays.

My family, bless 'um, thinks I'm dumb.

I scribble words upon this sheet

While there is nothing here to eat.

Real poets have no real income.

I could write some great country songs

On trucks, and trains, and loves gone wrong;

I'm real expert on broken hearted,

How does a lyricist get started?

If you know, call Bama after four...

Ask for that song writing Dinosaur.

James R. Ivey

Merger Proposition

You are at home in realms of gold,

Will you agree to be my guide?

I still get lost sometimes inside,

And need a wiser hand to hold.

Would you consent to be my muse?

If I should blend into your soul,

Surrender art to your control;

What would you risk that you can't lose?

Let's hitch your wagon to my star!

If you shared this inclination

We could be our inspiration;

Together, we could fly so far!

It's time for us to prove ourselves,

Or work at Wal-Mart stocking shelves.

My Job

If I could find the words tonight

To move some human soul or heart,

And make a smile – or tear drop – start,

I would have done my job… all right.

Poesy permits mystic insights,

We both can learn from what I do;

Old memories are shared with you

When they are sensed in poesy's lights.

Could I write the perfect sonnet?

Probably not… but should I care?

I don't believe I'd care to wear

Such a feather in my bonnet.

Science sails a perfect ocean…

I like salt with my emotion.

My Poems and Children

Writing a poem is like raising a child.

As a father, you hope they share your dreams,

But they have their own ideas it seems...

You plan a path. They prefer to run wild.

You learn that each has a will to survive,

They refuse to let you control their life;

I noticed that tendency in my wife...

They are not perfect, but they are alive.

I guess my duty is to get them started,

I can't help it if they pick their nose;

They will not allow me to choose their clothes...

Inadequacies leave me broken-hearted.

Perhaps, I'll soon be wise enough to know

They have their own lives...I must let them go.

My Reluctant Muse

I guess I could bring more flowers.

She loves the routines of romance,

But I only have life to dance...

I don't have time to waste man hours.

If I could hold her every day,

That would inspire sweet poesy's charms;

If she would lie within my arms,

Then I would know just what to say.

She could end my desperation.

But when I need her most, it seems,

Is when she will not share my dreams,

And will not be my inspiration.

Sometimes, she turns to me at night

With songs that make my music right.

Obituary

He was alive. Now he is dead.

He lived behind. Now he's ahead.

Some say he lived for wine and song,

And lovely ladies who lived wrong.

He had some virtues. Quite a lot.

But what they were we all forgot.

He walked real tall and knew no fear.

He had delusions of grandeur.

That was a lie. This is the truth:

When he was young he wasted youth.

In middle age, he was no sage.

Still, he put words upon a page.

He was a carrier of fire,

Who lies in ashes of desire.

Out of Season

Should strangers talk or should they touch?

Sometimes worn words get in the way,

And blur the truth life would convey...

"Come here!" she said. "You talk too much!"

Coming late and out of season,

Passions force a foreign feeling;

Sending conscience freely reeling...

Youthful fire burns up old reason.

The fire was in her fingertips,

Her breath, her perfume, and her hair...

I could have died and did not care!

She drank my will out through my lips.

As I recovered from deep delight:

"That was a poem...you should write!"

James R. Ivey

A Promise

My brother Orpheus sang such sweet words,

He charmed all the Gods and shamed the song birds.

Armed with Apollo's lyre and half-muse breath,

He boldly sang his love away from death.

And you, pale shadow, more fair than she,

Should you not expect even more from me?

When you left, I had not sweet voice nor charms

To lull the Gods who held you in their arms;

But years in passing have sweetened my song,

And I shall bring you back where you belong.

I will build you a castle in hearts of men,

And you, immortal, shall preside therein...

A castle with walls even Death can't climb...

A castle composed of meter and rhyme.

Scientific Impossibility

When things cannot be felt, the feel of things

Must grow -- Fortify your mind with poetry.

That golden bridle of antiquity,

And then awake to find your soul with wings!

Fly free of foolish fact that science brings.

Like God, touch all the stars men say must be

Much more significant than man, the flea.

Find peace in some soft vale where muses sing.

There are things science does not understand.

Man's gift of grafted growth is fact's cruel curse.

How tall is man? Quite tall enough to stand

Astride this scientific universe.

He reaches Heaven, with stars in his hand,

And can, with angels and with God, converse.

Thoughts and Feelings

I can't be another man,

Nor do I wish to be;

I must try to understand

Just who, on Earth, is me.

God gave me work with rhyme,

There's really too much of it,

But when I steal the time

God knows how much I love it!

I love to feel out thoughts,

Their touch is so appealing;

And when I have them caught

I love to think out feelings!

Thoughts and feelings here today,

If not loved, will go away.

Transformation

Just put a pencil in my hand,

And I become a different man;

I feel the rhythm of this Earth,

And sense the reasons for my birth.

Now, I can hear the Angels sing,

And see beyond old Saturn's ring;

As all my faculties unfold,

I sense some stories still untold.

To make these dreams reality,

God loaned poetic art to me;

Now I must speak to hearts of men

Before He takes it back again.

We all have promises to keep

Before death rocks us each to sleep.

James R. Ivey

Where are the Poets?

Do you know where the poets are?

Some slipped unseen beneath the sod,

Returned, unused, their gifts from God;

And never reached to touch a star.

Why not produce such sacred art?

Our age requires that all be fact,

Love and beauty are not exact;

Science cuts out a poet's heart.

Where do they hide then when they come?

They walk around in some disguise,

With no light shining in their eyes;

They may be ugly, but they're not dumb.

They have no choice in these cruel times,

When mad-house inmates speak in rhymes.

Why Be a Poet?

Why be a poet? You would ask?

To answer is no simple task.

We look for gems! We seek the truth!

For this, we sacrificed our youth.

We don't have time to darn our socks!

If we hauled garbage from four to two,

At least we'd know when we were through.

Success or failure? No one cares!

There's no market for metric wares.

If we were wise we would aspire,

To live out lives of less desire.

There's still a chance we'll go insane.

We have the courage! But not the brains.

Wild Choices

Perhaps my favorite recreation

Is riding my wild imagination;

For I never know where the trail will end,

Or when it may quickly start-up again.

Even though discipline's thought more clever.

I hope my wildness will last forever;

I like to ride through wide open spaces;

While thoughts run free to different places.

I can ride north to old bean town,

Or south for juleps in my cup;

Or east to see the sun come up,

Or west to watch as it goes down.

I can do things to be proud of,

Choose what I like and who to love.

Reminiscence

Hey!

Wake up to the real world

Where napkins and party plates

And cradles and coffins

Demand your sacrifice.

Once with regal majesty,

You towered toward heaven,

And stood as nature's prince.

But, that was yesterday.

Today, what's left, belongs to me.

Believe it. You will never see

A poem lovely as a tree.

Are you day-dreaming now?

Do you remember green hours,

And springs of song-filled boughs?

Do you long to embrace a cloud?

I have mad moments, too.

Forget it!

James R. Ivey

Book 2

Love's Embrace

James R. Ivey

Love Story

I loved you long before I knew

That God had made someone like you;

I loved a girl I thought ideal,

And then I found that you were real.

Can you imagine my surprise

When I first looked into your eyes?

I knew at once that it was you,

And that you were my dream come true.

The years have come and gone since then

While you've been both: Lover and friend;

Our children now are grown and gone,

But there's still fire when we're alone.

I remember your amused delight,

When I proposed that very first night.

James R. Ivey

Advice to a Young Man

To know a woman a man must live

Within the boundaries of her soul;

He must take what she will give

And add himself to make love whole.

Risk all for love: Heart, soul, and mind.

If you come close the music's sweet;

Put all you are upon love's line

The Angels sing when love's complete.

Suppose your efforts prove in vain?

Do not feel sorry for yourself!

The pleasure's always worth the pain

So, don't sit still upon life's shelf.

Love won't wait while you learn to dance,

So, cut in now, and take a chance.

Dancers I

When I was young I loved a girl

Who was the beauty in my world;

But I was shy, she never knew...

Too late I learned she'd loved me too.

When we were all but out of breath

She said a dream she brought to death:

With sadness, was I never came

To her window and called her name.

I was of Earth! She was a star!

I never dared to reach that far!

For shyness, youth must pay great cost,

For lack of courage love was lost!

I never learned about romance...

I was afraid to learn to dance.

Dancers II

When once I fell out of a boat

On our lake, and could not float;

Hers' were the arms that brought me back,

And saved me from Death's first attack.

"Now" she laughed, "You'll never be free!

All you become belongs to me!"

As I watched her from my safe shore,

All things were as they were before.

Later, she said, "Dance with me now."

"Sorry" I said, "I don't know how."

She danced with another named Jim,

And some years later she married him.

Can you ever go back again?

Life has some streets unknown to men.

Dancers III

If we could just go back somehow,

And take with us what we know now;

Would this world then turn about?

I rowed the boat, and then jumped out.

Her strong young arms brought me back,

And saved me again from death's attack;

"See" she smiled, "You never were free!

All you have been belonged to me!"

At her window, I called her name,

And life for us was not the same;

True love has its own melody,

Once you hear it you can't be free.

"Get up, dear girl! Where are my pants?

I think it's time I learned to dance."

Eager Arsonist

I love it when you flame desire,

Love's passions burning in your eyes;

I always feel such sweet surprise,

That I have started such wild fire.

A million years of style and grace

Now disappear in just one night;

There's no demeanor but delight

When passion rules a lady's face.

To quench such fire requires a flood,

A matching force for fire to meet;

And holding you can always heat

My English-Irish-German blood.

French ladies make a proper lover

When an arsonist goes undercover.

Fall

In the fall the trees are all on fire,

Nature paints pictures in our mind;

The burning leaves are our last sign

That we should stop and taste desire.

We always have somewhere to go,

And dreams to chase we think won't wait;

We are surprised, when it gets late,

To wake up dying in the snow.

Spring memories are small consolation

When summer bronze turns deathly white;

There are no fires to warm that night,

We enter alone with desperation.

Let's put this frantic life on hold,

And share this love we still control.

Fire and Ice

All young men seem to be on fire,

They have asbestos in their veins;

They're ruled by flesh and not by brains,

And live as slaves to love's desire.

It seems that nature, by design,

Makes young ladies queens of reason;

So, fire and ice share one season,

And she controls him with her mind.

Women tend to catch fire later.

Then it seems without rehearsal

There does occur some role reversal,

And she becomes love's generator.

What happens then when fire meets passion?

Some old love songs are back in fashion.

Flashback

Sometimes our memories will slip behind

The sunrise curtains of our current years

To times when love and faith and trust were new,

And no vows or promises lay broken.

Flashback is more than literary technique.

Two imperfect parts once came together,

For one sweet moment, and we learned heaven

Was much-much more than a madman's dreams.

This callous, mundane world ceased to exist...

There was just the two of us in paradise.

Just as you closed your eyes my soul fell in,

And fused with yours and we were one;

Together again in our lost garden

With no knowledge or fear of crawling snakes.

Good Bye, Marie

Her beauty and passion have claimed my heart.

Her charms have chained my soul...I am not free

To tarry...but tonight is ours, Marie...

Let's love ten years an hour! Then when we part,

Pains parting lovers feel should never start.

During days or dreams, don't think about me;

Woman's love can't keep a man from the sea.

She calls to me. I hear, and must depart.

In some forgotten time, man left first womb

Somewhere in sweet dark depths of sea, to roam;

But some must journey home to find their tomb

Where life was first conceived, beneath the foam.

My mind of late, has felt that final gloom...

I hear my mother's call. I must go home.

I Thought I Saw You

Today, I saw someone across the street,

And without thinking I called out your name.

She neither turned nor looked. I often meet

Someone whose form or face appears the same,

At first...then I look close enough to see

How unlike you she really is. My Dear,

Have you done that? Have you called out to me

"Where are you?" only to recall I'm here?

You ask of me? I keep busy all day...

But these long, lonely nights -- Dear God! I swear,

They're hard! I reach for you in that old way,

And wake up crying since you're never there.

My heart's still yours these years since you've gone...

When one lives with the dead...one loves alone.

James R. Ivey

Loving Smiles and Caring Eyes

A man who loves becomes a slave,

To his woman, his child, his art;

He is a hostage of his heart,

With no freedom outside his grave.

A man who cares has no defense

Against the vulgaries of life;

Earth's baseness cuts him like a knife,

Sorrow stalks him without pretense.

Emotions rule his waking hours,

Fear fills him: body, mind, and soul;

There's nothing here he can control,

Winter always kills the flowers.

The loving smiles do not disguise

Terror lurking in caring eyes.

Mind Games

I think of you more than I should,

I should not hold you in my mind;

But seeing you just feels so good,

And I'm a man who is not blind.

I guess it's time that I should go

On with this life you cannot share;

Perhaps you're lucky you don't know

How very much I really care.

I can't allow my love to show,

And if I stay it would but grow

Until my heart is on my sleeve

And it's too late for me to leave.

Still in my heart, I know I'll find

I'll always love you...in my mind.

Mud-Pies and Puppies

I remember when you

Were my mud-pie girl,

And I was your friend

From the puppy-dog world.

Can you remember, too,

The magic of that hour

(How shy we were back then!)

When love began to flower?

Forever is, it seems,

Only real in lands of dreams;

All love promised, in your eyes,

Proved forever...was all lies.

I still dream more than I should...

Mud-pies really can't taste good.

Needs I

A real man needs his woman near...

He needs her essence, to revere;

He needs her love to calm desire

When blood flows hot, like liquid fire.

When his world becomes a hostile place

He needs her softness, style, and grace;

He needs her beauty, brains, and charms,

He needs that comfort and surprise

When love burns hotly in her eyes.

I must march to my Maker's beat,

No man alone can be complete.

Where you walk now, my Eden goes,

But gardens here can grow a rose,

With seeds.

Needs II

I need your gifts to gain my goals,

I need the strength from our shared souls.

I guess it's true, I need a lot:

All that you are that I am not.

I need to give as much as take,

To pool our streams into one lake.

An absent lover leaves a space

No cards or letters can replace.

You need to know just how I feel:

If I can't hold you, you're not real.

"Absence makes the heart grow fonder."

Briefly. Then it makes it wonder.

I love you when I hold your hand,

But when I can't, I'm just a man with needs.

October Isolation

From here, I cannot see outside...

I can't see how our Southern trees

Are dancing with the Northern breeze...

And yesterday...more people died.

Frustration...and aggravation...

I can't see the clouds or sunshine;

I can't see new seasonal signs...

My October isolation.

Love is one thing I still can see,

That's something that I still can do;

Within my heart I can see you...

All that you are is clear to me.

Within my heart, and mind, and soul,

Your vision still has sweet control.

Old Fool

When you are young, you think you know

So much more than you really do.

But it takes years to learn that's true

For when you're young it's just not so.

Now I can see so many mistakes!

I should have been more understanding

With those I loved, and less demanding;

I could have saved so much heart-ache!

I feel I'm back in fifty-five,

The journey there is still a blur;

I talk to both myself and her,

I was young and she was alive.

"Who was that?" She wore the same dress.

"I don't know...some old fool, I guess."

Sadako

Her Asian beauty was so unreal,

One sultry look could make a proud man kneel;

I've seen her walk into a crowded room,

And fill every woman's heart with gloom.

Her musical movements, and form, and face,

Made a man memories time can't erase;

She was all pride, and poise, and sex appeal,

With no idea how rejection could feel.

Even though she was another man's wife,

I planned to teach her the dances of life;

She learned the dances too quickly and well,

And waits for me now in Heaven...or hell.

Music can be haunting when you're too wise,

The piano player has such sad eyes.

James R. Ivey

Space Objects

In some selected space in time two spheres

Collided: Souls were swept by sour-sweet flames;

Hearts burned to ashes by pleasures and pains.

They cried through smiles and laughed through tears.

While the lessons of love are never quite clear,

The graduate students are always the same;

When love burns your heart, and proves in vain,

You become more Monk and less Cavalier.

Funny how flames fall to mere sparks of fire,

And how some silly sparks refuse to die;

Funny how those sparks can flame back to desire

With the touch of a hand or wink of an eye.

Funny how long healing really requires...

So funny it hurts, and once more you cry.

Sumiko I

Once, in Japan, I found a diamond

In the mud of life's oldest profession.

When they brought the girls out for me to choose,

Her fragile beauty took my breath away,

And I could see no farther than her sad eyes.

I was young and lonely and very lost,

And she was older and wise and found me,

And I knew that there was no choice to make.

In the fleeting hours of that purchased night

She held me as tenderly as a bride,

And I loved her like she was forever,

And tangled our tears when the sunrise came.

We both knew that one night was not enough.

We dressed each other and left together.

Sumiko II

We rented a small house close to the bay,

In the shadow of the ship that owned me.

Each morning she would walk me to the pier,

Smiling sweetly as I held her soft hand.

She was waiting for me each afternoon,

And then the magic moments came again.

We had no common words for each other,

But none were needed to explain our love.

Sometimes in darker nights, I would awake

And sense her crying in lonely silence.

I would light up the lantern then and lie

Holding her safely away from the world,

Where love is a subject of time and tides.

Our weeks, like water, slipped through our fingers.

Sumiko III

She wrote a long letter after I left,

And my friends all laughed at my silly tears.

As the years come and go I am surprised

To find written there so much that is new.

When I am sad I find secret wisdom

In her strange lines that makes me smile again.

When I'm lonely I find some hidden phrase

That carries me back to those magic days.

When I am weak it is my source of strength,

And gives me the courage to go on living.

I will not translate the letter for you

Because translation spoils a lovely line,

And the language of love is personal.

Besides, I can't read a word of Japanese.

Their Story

They are only well known to each other.

He will never own a Rolls-Royce car,

And she will never be a Movie Star...

He's just a simple Father. She's a Mother.

He would not think an Angel above her.

She taught her boys how to sew and to bake...

He taught her boys how to fish in the lake.

He's an American Dad. She's his lover.

She's main street pleasure in his small-town life.

He taught their children all about fair-play,

And she taught them all how to kneel and pray;

He's her sweet treasure. She's his wicked wife.

In each other's arms, they find true glory.

They love each other well...that's their story.

Touch and Need

We don't touch much...and that not long;

All roads through life rush to the grave,

We ride the crest of one fast wave...

We should not sing a solo song.

Time is sadly in short supply;

If life was still at pre-flood length

We would have time to show some strength...

Do more than breed, and bleed, and die.

We must shape quickly, from our hearts,

Our world within and worlds without;

Let's give some love to those who doubt...

Life should not end before it starts.

We don't need much: Life is too brief...

Smiles are riches stolen from grief.

James R. Ivey

Tradition

Beauty, balance, and symmetry

Are all important things to me;

I love tradition's form and grace,

And melodies that flow in place.

I like Beethoven, Brahms, and Bach,

And art to please instead of shock;

I like to see my lady fair,

And not with curlers in her hair.

I do like nature very much,

But I do love the human touch;

I like song birds, but still my choice

For beauty is a woman's voice.

I love the beating of her heart,

And need that rhythm in my art.

Two Loves the Heart Holds Fondest

Two loves the heart holds fondest: first and last.

Not all the years that we can live apart,

Will be enough to free my foolish heart,

From fond memories of an unfading past.

My present love sighs with angelic breath.

Her love is sweet and warm; her heart is true.

Still in my sheltered moments, I think of you.

Our love will live inside me until death.

There is no breach of faith in how I feel.

My new love shall be the last of my love;

I could not have found a more loving wife.

But still, what we once had is no less real.

Sweet memories from and unfading past!

Two loves the heart holds fondest: first and last.

James R. Ivey

We Call it "Love"

Some men fight it, but there's no use,

Like a Hoover that runs in heat;

We suck up to new girls we meet…

We are compelled to reproduce.

Our silly selves and foolish friends,

Spend all our lives, and all we made;

In order that we might get laid…

We do not want our lives to end.

This ancient urge to propagate,

Has us holding pretty flowers

To swap for horizontal hours

with those we would inseminate.

A delusion that men seem most proud of

Some women differ. We call it "love."

Young Lovers

From you, I've learned that love is real,

I know it when I'm in your arms;

An eager captive of your charms,

With love the magic chains I feel.

A long road lies before us, Dear,

Long and filled with stormy weather;

Let us face those clouds together,

And treasure moments that are clear.

Give me your hand that wears my ring,

That golden circle I'm proud of

For it is eternal, like my love...

I'll need you... for everything.

Can we make it? Of course, we can!

Your love makes me a stronger man.

Reclamation Proclamation

I feel my bouncing belly on my belt,
And feel holes in my hair I've never felt;
This world weighs heavy upon my shoulder,
And seems to weigh more as I grow older.
I've come home late, a broken shell of man
That brought trouble and care in either hand;
I've come home late, with barely enough strength
To walk that last ten feet of driveway length.
But then small shapes in bright attire for sleep,
Laugh and shout and run about my tired feet;
And once again I feel sweet babies' charms,
And take them all, in turn, into my arms.
Then she is there, and she reclaims my life
With sweet warm kisses from a warm sweet wife;
Then a quiet dinner planned for just us two,
And the world is our pillow when we're through.
Cares are soon lost in love's consummation,
Troubles are drowned in love's deep sedation;
My belly still bulges, I've holes in my hair,
But then, I am a King...why should I care?

First Love

Sometimes, I slip and fall away

From the insanity of today,

To simpler moments in fifty-five

When downtown Dothan was alive,

And we were still unmolded clay.

Watching re-runs in black and white

In a movie house, as dark as night,

I sit and hold your lovely hand,

And think that life I understand.

Outside the day is harsh and bright.

Your lips were soft, until the lies

Brought that harshness to your eyes.

Our love was all a love could be,

There was just us, no you nor me.

Who knows where it goes when it dies.

Sometimes, I slip away through time

To a movie that costs a dime...

This time we are not so clever

That we can destroy forever.

I hold your lovely hand in mine...

James R. Ivey

The Eternal Triangle

The soft sensuous fingers of moist night wind
Caressed her...and found her unresponsive;
The sweet warm gusts were like his playful hands
When they would muss her perfect auburn hair...
But now she did not laugh...she could not laugh.
She walked so sadly...so slowly...conscious
Always of that thin sand border between
Her and her now hated adversary...
The sea! So dark, so deep...so eternal!
Now and then she could feel the enemy
Reaching out for her too, unsatisfied
With her victory...she felt the chill move
Through her blood and body as the icy
Fingers reached out, closed around her ankles
And then...so arrogantly! Retreated...

She had come here nightly since she lost him.
Magnetically, she was drawn back to this
Once bright and sunny, now dark and dreary
Beach that was the last place to share their love.

72

Now she knew...too late...that the hated sea
Had always been watching them, envious
Of their sure love and sweet happiness.
He had loved her as he had loved his life...
But he had also loved this jealous sea...
Blind to all its depth and dark deception.
The sea had always been her love rival,
Unknown, silent, but always...always there.
That ageless, faceless, formless foe whose arms
Had held so many before...now held him.
Now she heard the soft sea waves that muffled
Sadistic laughter and she cried again.

His lifeless shell had been thrown back to shore,
But the sea had retained the life and soul.
He had been taken from her just one month
Before this day...when she would be his wife.
She removed the too frail, the too modest
Girl's garments and went to join her husband.
In a golden gown of moon-light gossamer
She went as his bride to where he waited...
In the strong arms and dark depths of eternity.

73

James R. Ivey

Is That Clear?

———— ❧ ————

Somethings is, and somethings ain't;

Somethings can, and somethings can't;

But love is, and ain't, it both can and can't.

Now is that clear, to you, my dear?

Some say love, I heard, is a four-letter word;

But not to me, I just see three.

I hope you agree, on this, with me.

Is this all clear, to you, my dear?

Love wears a disguise for pedantic eyes;

It looks like four... it's less, not more.

I hope you agree the letters are three;

I and me, won't do, I spell love: Y.O.U.

An Acrostic Challenge

Long have I pondered humanity's state
Of war, pollution, poverty and hate;
Vainly I have asked a cure for these things
Even from peasants to great lords and kings.

Little is known by any that I see
Of a key in this life to set men free;
Very often I pray a key is near...
Each of us should seek a treasure so dear!

Let us all go in search across this sphere
Over mountain and plain, it must be near!
Very soon a day, which I pray we see,
Each of us happy, prosperous, and free.

Lay aside all else! Come search for the key
Of contentment and peace, for you and me;
Vain it may seem, but so well worth the time
Evil forgotten...an end to all crime.

The Moon's Wedding

The red roses were playing in the dew
With camellias white and violets blue;
Yet the garden's fairest flower that June
Was the girl who was there on her honeymoon.

The night was heavy, but her heart was light.
When he took her fair hand, she held his tight,
And looked to heaven at a wondrous view
For the Lady Moon was a new bride too!

This girl, so in love, saw a silver ring
Worn by the moon, and such a lovely thing;
She shared her happiness of wedded joy,
But her pure young heart belonged to the boy.

Sleep was elusive...and soon came the dawn,
Both the fairest flower and girl were gone;
A new woman rose and went out to see
If her new friend was as happy as she.

Her heart fell when she looked up to the sky,
And with tears of sadness she wondered why,
On this new morning, she was all alone;
Both her star and beautiful ring were gone.

Watching her move in a vast empty sky
The woman thought of lovers and good-byes;
Of paradise lost before it can grow.
Of life as it is, and why it is so.

"I am but a woman so far below.
I share your great sorrow...for well I know
How very tragic my own life would be
If my dear one should say 'Good-bye' to me."

She returned to his bed and did not speak
Planting sweet kisses on her gardener's cheek;
Then lay beside him afraid she might weep,
For sorrow must come as surely as sleep.

James R. Ivey

Advice to Youth

Your grass is green

Your sky is blue;

The birds and bees

Belong to you.

Your lakes, your streams,

Your stars above;

Live all your dreams

And fall in love.

Lost Love I

Once upon a happy time,

Not so very long ago,

In a land of sweet illusion,

Two young fools collided,

And love slipped softly

Between stupid fingers

Like Panama City sands

Through a broken hour glass...

This beautiful love,

Now shattered and scattered,

Drifts bruised and battered

On winds of immaturity.

Lost Love II

Just when I thought

I knew everything,

And had everything,

You left me with scars

That I can't explain

To that part of me

That will always be

In love with only you.

I guess I only saw

What I wanted to see,

Until you showed me

What was missing

Between my dreams

And your reality.

Lost Love III

I guess I'll go on

Trying to prove

That under ideal Circumstances

Two can become one,

And what's missing

In my completeness

Can be furnished

By someone, somewhere, Sometime.

I wish that I could see into tomorrow

Just as clearly as yesterday.

Would that feel as good

As this feels bad?

I wish right now

That forever...was.

James R. Ivey

Book 3

Life Reflections

James R. Ivey

Green Groves

There is a mirror in my mind.

There was a time that man I see

Reflected there, was really me.

He had good eyes, but he was blind.

You think you know more than you do

As you walk through green groves of youth;

The things you know are not the truth

As time, one day, will prove to you.

Your friends, and you, are all unique.

The world bows down before your reason,

And then you sense a change in season,

And watch close friends cut down like wheat.

Still, I wish I could move once more

Through those green groves we all adore.

Birthday, 1990

I'm forty-eight! I should prepare

A farewell speech to teeth and hair!

My ducks won't line up in a row,

It seems they have somewhere to go.

Do I dare to eat a peach?

Should I stand and make my speech?

This world won't listen anyway!

"What's he eatin'? What'd he say?"

For all the beauty in my life,

I thank my children and my wife;

I should apologize, I guess,

For leaving ya'll in such a mess.

There was so much I could not do!

We all say that. I guess it's true.

Circus

I ran away to be a clown,

The life looked magic to a boy;

But looks deceive and can destroy

When smiles are paint on upside down.

A flying girl with golden hair,

Once held my heart with earthless ease;

They slipped and fell from her trapeze,

And sawdust broke, beyond repair.

I watch with tears the tent come down...

Why can't we know where life will go?

The locals all have seen our show...

It's time to play some other town.

We leave nothing but wagon tracks,

Some empty dreams, and popcorn sacks.

Destiny's Child

Sometimes, a man may walk the street,

Who looks like most a man might meet;

Except...you sense a passing fire,

And feel the force of fame's desire.

You stand awe-struck in stunned surprise:

Such pure power! Such strange sad eyes!

"He's not like us" says your soul's voice,

"And what he is, is not his choice."

Destiny's child, ordained from birth,

To create history while on Earth;

Great good, or evil, is his fate,

To heal with love, or kill with hate...

Until, at last, he too must stand

With Ozymandias...in silent sands.

Gladys and Earl

All his children are coming home...

Like tumbleweeds on windblown sand;

They're scattered now throughout the land--

Ain't it funny how young folks roam?

Since Gladys died he's lived alone...

We played some checkers Sunday night.

He said his children never write--

And him without a telephone.

They all came home when Gladys died...

In that old lady lived a girl

Who was the sunshine in his world--

They hugged their Daddy, while he cried.

Earl was the best friend that I had...

He's back with Gladys now. I'm glad.

Harvest Time

I'm standing in this field alone,

A tired old man with work to do;

My neighbors now are all but through,

For harvest time is almost gone.

"You cannot reap more than you sow...

As sure as day shall follow night

All things buried will come to light."

I heard that somewhere...long ago.

I was young and scorned this season!

The blood that boiled so hot back then

Cost me dearly in love and friends...

I wonder now about my reason.

The kids are grown, and glad, and gone...

My wife prefers...to be alone.

Hourglass

I knew a man, this world called Brother,

Who held a thing for me to view,

"Imagine this" he said, "Is you."

The fertile shape looked more like mother!

"Now all your days are like this sand

That slips so surely through this glass;

As you, yourself, shall surely pass

Out of this life we understand."

Not true, I thought. Sand falls down, dumb,

And all I am aspires to rise

Up to some realm where men are wise,

And call me Brother when I come.

No life for me upon some shelf...

I'll break the glass and free myself!

James R. Ivey

Interview
(With the Alabama Dinosaur)

———————— ✖ ————————

Some of these questions are really hard!

My favorite writer is Lewis Grizzard.

I think Paul Newman is a charmer,

My favorite poet is Richard Armour.

I don't like politicians much at all,

But I'll always love Lauren Bacall;

I like the Braves, lose, lose, or lose,

And beer is still the drink I choose.

I think Sinatra has a fabulous voice,

But Reba McIntyre is my first choice;

I like some new folks now and then,

But still my son is my best friend.

Why does marriage end in divorces...

And why do bad guys buy slow horses?

Inventory, 1978

I'm thinking more about defection.

I'll leave these bills that I can't pay,

Garbage them all and go away;

My life, it seems, has no direction.

This harshness cuts me like a knife!

I dream of clouds, and harps, and such;

Perhaps, I'm dreaming way too much...

At least I have a pretty wife.

There are three kids somewhere about.

My girls show signs of being wise,

The boy has greatness in his eyes,

I guess I'll see how they turn out.

I hate a harp, and I can't sing,

And I'm too fat to fit the wings.

Legacy

Each man who lives leaves a legacy.

Sometimes, at night, when I'm alone,

I think with thoughts not quite my own;

My fathers still survive in me.

They lived and loved...they laughed and cried.

If I could learn from their mistakes

I could avoid some real heartaches;

They learned of life before they died.

All life they learned is in my genes.

If I were wiser in more ways

I might remember those yesterdays,

And figure out just what life means.

How far back go man's memories?

Those slimy snakes where in the sea!

Let's Love the Children

If we love all the children today

All world problems will soon fade away;

Let's show them love wherever they look,

Examples teach much better than books.

Let's plant some honor, courage, and pride,

And these worthy seeds will grow inside;

A smile, a hug, a real human touch,

These are the gifts they need so much.

Let's give them God and teach His lessons,

And all this world will share His blessings;

Let's help them grow with new confidence,

And then selfishness will not make sense.

The loveliest things in this poor world

Are happy faces of boys and girls.

Lions and Gazelles

———— ✣ ————

Each dawn, the mighty lion stretches.

Massive muscles made for killing...

Ancient appetites need fulfilling.

He holds no hate for what he catches.

He knows that his staying alive

Requires he kill some slow gazelle;

The fleet gazelles all know too well

Their slowest kin will not survive.

Sunset -- another chapter's read

The running, for today, is done;

For some, the final race is run...

Those slow gazelles and lions are dead.

And now here comes the rising sun:

Are you ready to rise and run?

Poverty and Me

Poverty is a friend of mine,

We've been together since my birth;

He holds my feet upon this Earth,

And proves to me that things aren't fine.

When I allow myself these dreams,

He wakes me up with cold hard fact;

Why must our lives be so exact?

We are too practical it seems.

I don't need much: paper and pen,

A little luck to pay the rent;

The landlord says, "It's time ya'll went",

And we're back on the road again.

Our suitcase is a K-Mart sack...

But it don't take us long to pack.

97

New Kid

The new kid on the block is me.

How much longer can I do that?

My shoes are worn, and so's my hat,

But still I move when I'm not free.

Circumstance can own a man

If he surrenders to one place;

So I will wear a stranger's face,

Before I kneel where I can't stand.

I'm not a man who is for sale.

Before I compromise myself,

Become an item on life's shelf,

I'll leave it all, and move to hell.

All that I am is what I know...

I can't afford to let that go.

Space and Time

Can two men occupy one place?

It seems I marched beyond my pace...

My mirror shows a stranger's face!

Who is that standing in my space?

Because I've left so much undone,

My mind still thinks I'm twenty-one;

My eyes tell me that's just not true,

That fat old geezer there is you!

I never heard the starter's gun...

How can you say my race is run?

With accomplishments, far too few,

It's time to reap what seeds I grew;

It's time to show what I can do...

A man should start before he's through.

Prejudiced

Nature's love of blue and green

Is seen in everything.

Look up. See the sky of blue?

She gave that to me and you.

She has some Irish soul,

She will not worship gold.

Let's color green to start

Your black-soul and my white-heart.

Sparrows deplore black-of-night,

Robins abhor winter white.

All nature's song-birds sing

Much sweeter in the green.

The Big Trade
(Random Thoughts, 30th Birthday, May 3, 1972)

They moved Willie from the Giants to the Mets!

Say, hey! If they can move a Willie Mays

What chance have I to grow any roots?

I suspect the Washington Monument

Will be traded to Brooklyn, for a bridge

And an undisclosed number of gold bricks.

These moves are minor in comparison:

The generation teams just traded me!

Before I leave, one last press conference:

Yes! Yes, this comes as quite a shock to me.

I never thought the establishment team

Would be interested in getting me.

We had a real long-running rivalry.

Yes. I feel sure that I can contribute.

Let's play two...

Going

Someone asked "Where are you going?"

And I said, "Just down to the store."

But that's not entirely true...

An easy answer for an indifferent ear.

How can one know where he's going?

If I knew where I was going

I might even learn who I am...

Who, and perhaps finally...what.

Does anyone know who he is?

Does anyone know what he is?

Does anyone have time to learn?

"Yes" my friends will say, "I know him well."

But that's more convention than truth.

I know as much about myself

As anyone--Yet there is much

Still left for me to discover.

I'm a puzzle with missing pieces.

I may find one somewhere today,

Perhaps on the way to the store,

And be one step closer to knowing.

I find them in the strangest places

When I least expect to find them.

Sometimes I am pleased by pieces I find.

Sometimes the pattern takes a frightening turn…

"I am going to look for myself."

Secrets

Ah, soft feline friend, what strange secrets lie
Concealed in the depths of your emerald eyes?
Do you know those secrets of life and death?
And the real fate of man with his last breath?

Tell me, Tough Tom, where you go in the night.
Just down dark alleys in search of a fight?
Or still farther on, to much stranger lands
Past all this world's alleys and garbage cans?

Have you ever stalked through eternity
And seen many things that I'll never see?
Have you sat, in God's lap, like this before,
And from His wise words learned even more?

Ah! I really wish that you would talk,
And tell me today about last night's walk;
Now why are you purring so rhythmically?
Please tell me, wise friend, just what do you see?

Something Fishy

A wise man of wealth caught a magic fish,

Who bartered his freedom for one wish.

"If you will tell me what I wish to know

I promise on my honor I will let you go."

The question he asked with short baited breath:

"Does a man ever know life after death?"

"Wise Sir, I freely swear my sacred vow,

You shall be as alive as you are now!"

Said the freed fish with diabolical mirth:

"You should have asked: Have I life here on Earth?"

Young Man's Spring

With wildly contagious enthusiasm,

Spring rushed in singing with gifts and flowers,

And soft warm showers, sweet and silver tasting,

That washed the weary weeks from Earth's old eyes.

She danced to death those dreary days of sadness,

And startled our slow star to wary warmth.

Splashing seas of blue-green throughout the scene,

She sewed dry-cleaned leaves back on naked trees.

My soul then bloomed like the fresh new flowers.

Ripped free by such wild glee my heart leaped up,

And joined in lilting song and blissful flight

Ten thousand free spirits that spring uncaged.

We soared away on sweet scented West winds

To love's lofty peak in lost paradise.

From that perfect peak of pure perception,

That not even God's Angels can rise above,

With Spring as our Sponsor, we surrendered to love.

Old Man's Spring

Spring is looking cool.

Outside, the wicked world wears camouflage,

And lunacy welcomes this cruel mirage.

Bees buzz too dumb to feel something is unreal.

The stupid robins sing, suckered by the green.

The young lovers are blind to nature's disguise.

They laugh at death, and believe foolish lies.

April shouts in Irish green: Life is King!

Very much like a dunce I joined in once.

"How beautiful April is!" I cried.

And while I grinned all living things died.

Spring is very much like a madman's dreams,

Seldom what he sees and never what it seems.

After silver showers fall death devours all.

Sound incredible? Nothing left is edible.

Life is nothing, not a thing. Death is King.

And April...is a fool!

107

James R. Ivey

Abridged Autobiography
Dothan, 1952

School was where you went during the day

Because bigshot politicians made you,

And where your lucky parents never went.

Home was where you slept during the night

In a big bed that was full of people

Because if it wasn't cold outside, it

was most likely raining. Love was what the

Giggling girls who were always laughing about,

And the thing your parents never mentioned.

A boy can get lost in a family

Of twelve, without his even trying to.

You wonder if anyone ever had

A brand-new shirt or shoes that were never

Ever worn by somebody else before.

You wonder if perhaps someday you might

Save enough (or steal enough) pennies

Daydreams

To buy yourself a real bait of ice cream.

You wonder why your mother always cries

When you try to ask about your brother

Who died long before you were ever born,

And you feel like it may have been your fault.

You wonder why your father has sad eyes.

You wonder why the electric people

Are always coming to turn off your lights.

And why sometimes, if you are very late

Getting to the table, there's nothing left.

Sometimes, if you're first, you might get away

With a whole fried chicken leg and maybe

A big handful of French fried potatoes.

Sometimes, if you're lucky, that might happen.

Later, you wondered how some silly girl

Could smile at you and stop your beating heart.

You wondered at a lot of things, but most

Of all, you wondered who you were...and why.

We Stand Alone

Life is a special spark in space.

Loose lights within the cosmic whole,

Combine to form a human soul…

An accident of time and place.

A miracle of blood and bone!

We lie helpless from our birth,

Until it's time to rule this earth…

Then like our Gods, we stand alone.

Rain
(A Better Biodegradable Detergent)

There have been times,

I've stopped and stood

In God's sweet tears.

Nothing else I've found,

Is quite as good

To cleanse my fears.

James R. Ivey

Book 4

Into the Light

James R. Ivey

Morning Prayer

Good morning, Lord! So glad You're here!

Now there's nothing that I should fear!

Open my eyes so I will see

The things that You desire from me.

Come walk with me throughout this day,

And guide my steps along life's way;

Please make me loving, pure, and true,

And gentle in the things I do.

Help me live! I can't walk alone!

Turn stumbling blocks to stepping stones!

Our lives are brief and quickly past,

But what we have, with You, will last.

So walk with me until I'm through,

And then I will...walk Home with You.

Banners

Eternal truths that men must know:

No Earthly wealth has saved one soul.

Man's worth is weighed in deeds, not gold;

Go share His gifts if you would grow.

We are His banners in this world;

Ecstasy belongs, tomorrow,

To those that spend to save some sorrow;

Don't let sun set on flags unfurled.

All Earthly things will pass away...

When you consider what you need

Remember grief will follow greed,

And spirits blessed will not decay.

God blesses those who share His Love...

Forever fits them...like a glove.

Book

This great Book, called life, should be closely read

Studied page by page before we are dead;

Life's laughter, and love, and purpose are there

As well as life's vengeance, sorrow, and care.

From each daily page, there's much to be learned,

But the sheets grow short and so quickly turned;

That soon we read there is no tomorrow...

With what we've retained we face this sorrow.

Only then do we know, too late indeed,

That while we were here, our purpose to read,

We touched, without holding, His Holy Creed.

Winter chills cry out for truth's sweet ember

Truths we forget we most need to remember.

Truth lights the soul in life's dark December.

Command Me

Jesus, I kneel before you now

Command me and I will obey;

I taste the blood upon Your brow,

And feel how much Your burdens weigh.

Show me what You will of me,

I am Your Servant and Your Son;

Command me. I will not be free

Until Your Holy tasks are done.

Because of you, I am, today,

And all I am I owe to you;

Send me, Lord, Upon Your way,

And I will see this journey through.

I am Your Pilgrim here on Earth,

Looking forward to second birth.

Conversion

What must a man do to survive?

This world is harsh. You must be tough.

Still all you do is not enough...

Nobody here...gets out alive.

Is our one purpose then, to die?

No! Man must learn, and love, and live;

All sons of God have much to give,

Each child who crawls can learn to fly.

How can we make our lives worthwhile?

Be a force for love and reason...

Be a light throughout your season,

And be a source of joy and smiles.

Each man who lives can change this earth...

That was God's reason for your birth.

James R. Ivey

The First Stone

I saw them standing close at back yard fence,

Wild tongue to wide ear with glee and suspense;

Neighborhood gossip is too often true,

But I am not perfect...neither are you!

Seeing me then on my evening walk

Brought a slow sad silence to joyous talk;

I passed on by with just a friendly nod,

But was tempted to ask which one was God.

Only God has rights to judge your brother,

He told us to love, not hurt, each other.

Why do some souls spend their few hours on earth

Working as mid-wife for cruel rumors birth?

If you will help me hide the sinner's stone,

The lives that we save, could well be our own.

Fraternity
(Student's Prayer)

Lord, make me wise enough today

To learn all things that I should know;

Show me the way that I must go

If I would live this life, your way.

Lord, help me love my fellow man,

Teach me now my Christian duty.

Help me know your truth and beauty,

And live my life the best I can.

Thank you, Lord, for this my chance,

Great teachers are Your gifts to me;

Where I was blind they make me see,

My worth, by knowledge, is enhanced.

When I have earned my last degree,

All that I am... I pledge to Thee.

I Had a Dream

I saw Earth's people peaceful and praying,

And all our children singing and playing;

Everywhere I looked His Love reigned supreme,

Thank God, Almighty! I had a sweet dream.

All of God's children had plenty to eat,

Clothes for their bodies and shoes for their feet;

Life's pilgrimage was fulfilling and sweet,

The honey of His love flowed through the street.

No one harming or hating another,

Each person felt each man was his brother;

All men of all colors all on one team,

Reality starts, sometimes in a dream...

Envy and evil had ended it seemed,

Thank you, Lord Jesus! I had me a dream!

Miracles

While I sat waiting for my muse,

Jesus came into my heart;

He said I had no time to lose,

And that He would inspire my art.

My mind became a fertile ground,

And His this harvest of my soul;

The form, the content, and the sound:

Baskets of silver -- Apples of Gold!

How quickly now my work is done

In ways that I don't understand;

I thank you Father, for Your Son,

Who helps to guide my human hand.

Are there Miracles in our age?

Let he who doubts, deny this page!

New Town, Same Boy

There are those times when a man looks back.

Twelve years ago, without much warning:

"I want you there by Monday morning!"

My job demanded that I go pack.

Like gypsies leaving a carnival town,

Me and my family were on our way;

With U-Haul trailing a Chevrolet,

We got 'there' Saturday well past sundown.

Much after midnight we went to bed,

And I had dreams of a dear one dead;

Waking up frantic I searched around...

My eight-year-old could not be found!

He walked in later proud as could be:

"I went out and found a church for me!"

Poet's Prayer

Dear Lord, I know you have a plan

For faith and works from every man;

I wear the poet's purple vest,

And by Your love my hand is blessed.

I know you placed within my heart,

This need to toil with ancient art;

Please help me learn and teach for you,

Your lessons that are always true.

Inspire that process in my mind,

That lets me see where men are blind;

Help me, Lord! This is my duty:

Lovely lines of truth and beauty.

Put perseverance in my soul:

Words of silver and thoughts of gold.

James R. Ivey

Salvation Army

The Architect of your life's plan,

Worked with patience, and worked with love;

His wish was that you build a man,

That He, and you, could be proud of.

He put this day within your power,

Pray that His will be done by you;

Go live and work within this hour,

And Heaven waits when you are through.

So, be the best that you can be,

A soldier for the common good;

When muster sounds eternally,

You too will stand where saints have stood.

His legions need leaders today...

He who commands must first obey.

Time Management

Make the most of every hour today,

For yesterday belongs to history,

And tomorrow is still a mystery

With Heaven, or hell, a heart-beat away.

Treasure each hour as a gift of God's love.

Procrastination's a spiritual crime;

You are wasting your life when wasting time,

For time is the thing your life is made of.

Meet daily troubles with determined fire,

And out of every adversity

Will come another opportunity,

For hope is the flower of man's desire.

So, start and end each new day with prayer,

Be strong and true; show your Lord you care.

Volunteers

Our kingdom is in need of all good men,

The brave and generous, the strong and true;

Only those who give their all will do,

Forces of darkness are marching again.

If you believe in law and loyalty,

Become a soldier for forces of light;

Defeat evil with love, and wrong with right,

Conquer oppression and hypocrisy.

We need volunteers who will all go the length:

Fight for the great cause that needs assistance,

Against the evil that needs resistance,

Serve with courage, nobility and strength.

Paths to eternity that saints have trod,

Await brave men from the Kingdom of God.

Search for a Friend

He climbed to the top of the big oak tree,
And he perched quite precariously there;
But he was still blind to what he would see,
Although he twisted and looked everywhere.

He looked from the hill crest, not seeing yet,
He then searched the river's long secret shore;
And other lost places small boys forget,
Until darkness would let him look no more.

Then he hurried home to warm food and bed,
And asked his mother, "Is our God away?"
She puffed up a pillow for a tired head,
And with wise loving words began to say,

"Our God is more than we see or hear,
Though He is our Father and more than real
He will not leave, He will always be near,
To love and watch over your life my dear."

Reunion

There kneeled an ancient soul in faithful prayer:
"Dear Lord, somehow this life just doesn't seem fair.
My world without her is worse than a tomb!"
And the wind moved softly outside his room.

"Please, Oh Lord! Won't You please send for me?"
Begged the tired old man on one crippled knee;
"Lead me through darkness with Your love's light,
So that I can see my Angel tonight.

Don't think I'm ungrateful for all we had,
I know you gave us more good times than bad;
It's just that my life is already gone,
A man's not alive when he's left alone.

I thank you for that time when life was fun,
And days were welcome when the night was done;
But now, my Lord, since you have her with you,
There ain't nothing here to look forward to.

I don't take much room. I don't eat too much.

I know I'm a bother 'cause of this crutch;

But she'll help me up there! You know that's true!

I bet if you ask her, she misses me too.

Though she thought your Heaven a real nice place,

She got real used to this ugly old face;

She saw it so much for so many years..."

Then tired voice stopped and old eyes became clear:

There before him was God. And she was there!

Gold for that silver now shined in her hair,

He ran to her with the vigor of youth,

The crippled old man...no longer the truth!

James R. Ivey

Book 5

Historical Satire

James R. Ivey

Lost Lips

Abe Lincoln read by candle light,

Most children now can't even read;

They just take what they think they need,

And watch T.V. every night.

The politicians have their way.

Collectively, without a brain,

They are too dumb to be insane,

We owe one trillion we can't pay.

This is my country, right or wrong!

Poverty's hell, you can't escape,

We lead this world in murder and rape;

We need to learn a different song.

It seems our problems have no grips,

Our President has lost his lips.

James R. Ivey

Cain and Us

Cain was the oldest son of Eve.

If Genesis can be believed,

He was the father of us all...

Did he meet 'mother' at the mall?

Cain murdered his only brother!

Still, somewhere, he found our mother.

Those frequent times we act insane...

Let's blame them all on father Cain!

And what of that curse Cain carried?

Did that end when he was buried?

Some say that man is never free

Of Darwin's urge to climb a tree.

Was there a time when you and I

Were lusty gleams...in a monkey's eye?

Clever Devils

Education is sadly funny...

No one learns and no one teaches

God forbid that someone preaches.

We get less for lots more money.

We've taken God out of our schools,

Nine old men say he's illegal;

They have the horse sense of a beagle,

And all are forced to follow fools.

Man, is now at new low levels,

We teach no morals to the masses;

Without religion in our classes

We graduate some clever devils.

The lambs of God don't get much sleep,

Schools turn out wolves to slaughter sheep.

James R. Ivey

Death of the Big-Shot Banker

The verdict is death when life is on trial,

So, at sixty-three, the town banker died;

The best actors in town assembled and cried,

While former land owners openly smiled.

He looked at the poor down a gold-rimmed nose,

As he raced through life pursuing his money;

Were it not so tragic it would be funny,

He defaulted on life and death foreclosed.

What were the great treasures he gained from life?

Ten sons, a mansion, and five lovely wives;

His greedy worthless sons long wished him dead,

And five former farmers warm his old beds.

From a lifetime of pride, envy, and greed,

Death finds us with nothing we really need.

Forever

They watched him grow with pure delight,

His father's joy right from the start;

With love to warm his mother's heart.

He always talked to God each night.

He grew up proud and tall and straight,

His honor could only increase

For he loved freedom more than peace.

Tyranny was the thing to hate.

His country called and he was gone...

That farewell was too brief, it seems,

And it dims daily in their dreams.

They lived together. He died alone.

Are there sadder words than never?

Today, he's twenty-one...forever.

Goddess of Good

The princely savage in primal wood

Knew freedom as the Goddess of Good.

When we were young, my nation and me,

We both decided we would live free...

With hopes (and fears!) and dedication;

We started free of obligation...

But now we've learned to our great regret

Freedom requires an absence of debt.

Today, this nation owes a trillion!

My own dumb debts must be a million!

We're prisoners in capitalistic chains...

We have no freedom, no life, no brains!

We create new Gods that we don't need,

And sacrifice our Goddess to greed.

Hard Times, Lean Dogs

When times are hard and dogs are lean,

Join the party, and you'll get elected;

No scoundrels have ever been rejected,

A man can prosper when he's keen.

There's not that much you need to do,

Remember that voters have no horse sense;

They never can tell a man's on a fence,

They think they're eating grass with you.

The parties will present your cases:

"Here are two rats who want your cheese,

Now you must choose which one you please,

They both have each two honest faces."

My father gave me advise that lingers:

"If you shake hands…better count your fingers."

Internal Revenue 'Service'

The letter came to my address,

The mail man had a form to sign;

It looked official by design,

And stated boldly: IRS.

I thought there must be some mistake,

But the letter said send money;

Someone there was thinking funny,

A man can't send what he doesn't make!

I went straight down to tell them that,

And I explained about my luck...

"Business losses took my last buck!"

But you can't talk to bureaucrats.

What they must mean by 'service' now

Is what a bull does to a cow.

Invaders

I dream I'm back in my ancient land.

A lady with never-ending charms

Awakes old memories in my arms...

War ships are mooring beyond the sand

A time for dying is close at hand.

Is the sentiment merely clever?

Or does love sometimes last forever...

I see burning ships from where we stand.

A man's not meant to know, it seems,

Just what is real and what but dreams.

"Thou was supposed to come" she said,

"One thousand years...I thought thee dead!"

A voice behind me, ghostly low...

"Captain! Captain! It's time to go!"

James R. Ivey

The Last Eagle

Truth lies holed up with the last bald eagle

In a cold Colorado canyon cave;

And they both refuse to come out again...

The atmosphere outside is filled with hate.

The old eagle made one last search for hope,

And saw only evil and envy and death;

Now they huddle in panic, holding their breath,

And they scream when startled by the thunder.

They are familiar with endangered species

They will not negotiate a treaty

With a world that thinks with forked tongue.

From their vantage point, they can always see

Stampedes of buffalo bones, bleached by the sun,

With gaunt Indian ghosts hot on their trail.

Leaving

I won't stop to debate with you,

There's too much madness in the air;

And apathy, but I don't care...

I'm just a guest and passing through.

'Lost lips' has launched a thousand ships,

And sent poor kids to bake and broil;

Mobile and Chevron need that oil

To stack new profits to their hips.

I think I'll go to Greece or Rome,

I can't feel safe here any hour;

Death won't wash off in the shower.

Don't call me up! I won't be home.

God bless Standard and God bless Shell!

God help our boys who are in hell.

James R. Ivey

Let's Build a Better World

News headlines blare: MURDER and RAPE!

Our Nation's madness seems complete…

No one is safe on Sodom's streets.

Is there no way we might escape?

Newspaper columns say our schools

Contribute little to tomorrow;

Our world is filled with pain and sorrow,

We march as dunces led by fools.

How can we build a better world?

First of all, good people could start

To redesign the human heart,

And build some better boys and girls.

Love cures corruption, hate, and crime…

Let's let Christ rule, while there's still time.

National Ethics, 1990

Preoccupied with their personal greed,

Our people abandon ethics and truth;

Honesty and respect are foreign to youth,

Whatever they want they think that they need.

When ethical pride is not being taught

In either the homes, the churches, or schools,

The idiots now are teaching the fools.

Like politicians, we all can be bought.

Television teaches all have the right

To success and comfort without any skill;

Those with nothing are mad enough to kill.

How many people were murdered last night?

Today, it seems, our nation is insane...

A big stupid body without a brain.

James R. Ivey

National Dance

We've learned to live without our pride,

We're the victims of nine old fools

Who've wrecked our rights and ruined our schools,

And divided us all on different sides.

Just look around you'll see the signs,

Internal conflict never ceases;

Morals are dying as crime increases,

Ours is a nation in quick decline.

Politicians are pawns of the wealthy.

That rich elite who own this nation,

And take without an obligation.

Poor people perish so they stay healthy.

We must learn a dance besides limbo...

We've gone as low as we can go.

On Hearing Richburg Defend America

What manner of man, I ask you, is this?

How can he forgive...how can he forget...

Then defend this great land, wherein he met,

Dark days and dead dreams from dumb prejudice?

What man who heard his noble heart could miss

Feeling the fool to be found in his debt?

Was there one who heard who does not regret

His own heart's silence...his own cowardice?

This man is black! Yet, in that learned crowd

His voice rose alone, and dared to defy.

I should have spoken first and twice as loud!

Yet held my stupid tongue...to wonder why.

That man's a great warrior, noble and proud.

Now what manner of man, Dear God, am I?

James R. Ivey

Pray and Prepare

Pray for peace and prepare for war...

Our freedom never has been free,

Our strengths preserve our liberty.

History has proved all this before.

Freedom requires some men must die...

Thousands of good men chose the grave

To peaceful living as a slave.

Is the price for freedom too high?

Some 'Americans' say that's true...

They protest that all wars should cease,

By burning 'rags'...red, white, and blue.

Slaves surrender freedom for peace.

The tyrants are watching our shore...

Pray for peace. Get ready for war.

150

Santiago

"A man can be destroyed, but not defeated."

He has in his heart, a God-given will,

And when strength of body and mind are depleted

He cannot surrender...he must be killed.

Like all lesser ladies our God created,

Our most ancient mother would not be cruel;

But moods of LaMar are moon-mandated,

And trust in lunacy makes dead men of fools.

Forgive me, Father! I have killed my brother!

I wasted his flesh and blood in the sea.

It was fate's choice. She allowed no other.

When he took my bait, it became destiny.

I rest...Your spirit is renewed, in me,

By dreams of young lions who play by the sea.

Second Coming

Perhaps the Second Coming is at hand?

Islamic idiots, heartless and cruel,

March mindless behind a leader of fools...

A repulsive monster, not kin to man.

Upon desert sands in the Middle East,

People are dying in an ancient land;

In this battle, between Devil and man,

Forces of honor are facing the beast.

It moves toward Bethlehem for new birth,

But the beast will be stopped, captured, or killed;

Evil ambitions will not be fulfilled,

For this slouching beast must not rule our earth.

This monster will die believing the lies:

Good lacks conviction...evil never dies.

That's Greek, To Me

When I see someone burn our flag

It makes me mad enough to kill;

Thousands have died and more still will

For what 'The Court' has made a rag!

Dead Americans pass in review...

They were all young, and proud, and brave,

And took Old Glory to their grave;

Brief lives faded like morning dew.

Don't we still have some obligation

To those who gave all that they had?

Can't we tell when justice goes mad?

Where is the conscience of this Nation?

Jefferson's English, as we speak,

Has been re-written into Greek!

James R. Ivey

Tinsel-Town Cowboy

— ❧ —

I used to ride the silver screen,

Where good guys never lost a fight;

That was the rule in black and white

For stars like Sunset, Lash, and Gene.

Wearing white hats we did our duty.

Our horses danced like Fred Astaire;

Wherever we went...big bands were there!

From Black Bart, we saved the beauty.

We kissed the girl then rode away.

Sarsaparilla was our main juice;

We did not stay to reproduce...

There are no good guys left today.

I'm not so sure I still know how

To punch a horse...or ride a cow.

154

Trojan Trilogy I

Am I the master of this bark

With which I plow life's dark-deep waves;

Or has some course for me been marked,

Charted by bones lost-long to graves?

Are these my father's ghosts in me,

That seem to plot my destiny?

Am I the man my world has known,

Or still the seed from which I've grown?

Today, I stand on this strange shore,

and feel my blood has flowed before;

I know this field where comrades cried,

Upon my grave, when once I died.

Now standing here, how much I missed!

The taste of lips…I've never kissed.

Trojan Trilogy II

The taste of lips…I've never kissed

A taste that death could not erase;

Misty memories from time's abyss,

Bring visions forth of form and face;

I see her then, that day I cam,

To this strange land in search of fame;

I feel the perfume of her breath,

That lingers still beyond our death.

Mother, lover, mistress, and wife,

With me all objects of her life;

Father and son, we both were one,

So one remained, when one was done,

To find this final place again:

"The Child is Father of the Man."

Trojan Trilogy III

"The Child is Father of the Man,"

We are still seeds which we have sown;

We often find in some new land.

We think with thought not quite our own…

We leave a print on some new shore,

And feel we've walked that beach before;

I sense, then see, with some surprise,

Confusion in a stranger's eyes:

"Have we met, sir?" I ask the man,

"Perhaps in another time, or land?"

"I think not, comes his slow reply,

Here I was born, here I will die…"

And then he takes a mad man's start:

"You threw the spear, that pierced my heart!

James R. Ivey

Twentieth Century Sonnet to History

Time is a rushing roaring river, with man

Just foolish flotsam, on flickering foam.

Floating pell-mell to his own private hell,

Which history shrouds from idiot eyes.

The far shorelines of days are blurring the graves,

Of righteous refuse rejected before

We float laughing and then crying

We drift dancing to our dying

All our dreaming and scheming,

Will cease forever with our screaming,

And our poor pious pleas for breath,

Are silenced forever with our death.

Still that roaring river rushes on, and man,

Is mindless flotsam, on flickering foam.

A Conversation on War

Go forth, child of nation. Feel nothing.

Just kill to fulfill your national obligation.

What's that you cry? Afraid to die!

But you owe that to our nation. What!

You're wondering why You're indebted to die?

Stop! Just Go forth with sword and gun.

And never come back less breath be gone

or freedom's victory won.

What's that you dare say? High price to pay!

For millions it was not!

The eager boys and dads

All were glad to give their very life!

High price indeed. They all said not!

True sir. But ask the weeping mother,

Or the mourning wife.

Sir, they say it is a lot.

They wonder and ponder and truly care,

And they too may even dare to ask of you, why?

You statesmen do the quarreling,

But it was her young man you sent to die…

James R. Ivey

Until the Conversion

—— ❧ ——

There were four yellow bodies and one black,

All tangled up in the machine gun nest.

The southern sergeant shook with angry tears,

"Blew his self to hell…with his own grenade!

Captain…why'd the boy do such a foolish thing?"

"That 'man' just saved all our lives, sergeant."

"But he had no right...to save my life…why?"

"We're all in this thing…together," he said.

Ode to Literary Critics

I am thrilled.

I am filled with divine strength and power.

I've debated, created and inflated a world in a hour.

What say you? For justice that be too quick?

Constructive criticism? Hogwash!

Be gone you prick - you make me sick!

Thought, you cry, is not there? Who are you?

Say what you will, I do not care.

You moan and groan and carry on

About mood and imagery? I've had all I can take.

Go jump in the lake! Just stay away from me...

I sweat and fret stubborn will to mold and build.

Now you're crying cheat and raving deceit.

Well, I have had my fill.

You say what success I know is luck,

That all I try doth run amuck.

Well, I'm tired of it, oh Hypocrite!

I give your garbage to the city truck!

Maid of Orleans

From Domremy in Lorraine, France,

There came a farmer's child;

A teen-age lass in male attire,

Whose eyes were slightly wild.

To aid the dauphin Charles, she came,

So he might claim his throne;

"The Saints are with me" she explained,

"I do not come alone."

At Patay, France, she led the French,

The English ran away;

One hundred years of bloody war

She brought to end that day.

She stood by Charles as he was crowned,

Her pure heart filled with pride;

Her king had claimed his rightful throne,

And she was at his side.

But most ungrateful wretch was he!

Still damned by Heaven's choir;

They sing of how he willed a saint

To bear the cross of fire.

James R. Ivey

Ballad in Blue and Grey...And Black

Through Shenandoah, North they rode

In June of Sixty-three,

The brave young men in garb of gray

Led by Robert E. Lee.

Fresh from Athena's warm embrace

They rode to war with pride;

Convinced their cause was just and right

And God rode at their side.

At Gettysburg, they faced the foe

Those brave young men in blue,

Who also knew their cause was just

And God rode with them too.

Daydreams

The cannon roared, the horses screamed,

Rivers ran red that day;

The Nation's pride lay dead and dying

When the smoke had cleared away.

Blue or grey, which did God favor?

Their women all wore black,

And no belief, however just,

Can bring their young men back.

James R. Ivey

Book 6

The Shadow Self

James R. Ivey

Adam and Eve

There was a brief moment in world history

When that one man on earth was truly free.

Young Adam was living that perfect life

When God decided...he needed a wife!

With rib-stubs stolen from Adam's own breast,

He framed our first mother. You know the rest.

Eve turned out lovely, but filled with deceit...

Adam had to have her to be complete.

She quickly had Adam under her spell,

Evicted from Heaven, both moved to hell;

They had one son followed by another...

The first grew up and murdered his brother.

Living with our Eves and raising our Cains,

It's a wonder more men don't go insane.

James R. Ivey

Alabama Dinosaur

Some new species of an ancient beast

Has been observed in the new Southeast;

I saw it falling from off life's wall

Beneath some gibberish it had scrawled.

It has not learned how to make ends meet,

And lives too close to Poverty street;

They say it finds perverse enjoyment

Subsisting on state unemployment.

Look! Right there! Behind that screen of smoke!

Can you not hear it? It coughs and chokes!

What a horror for the world to see!

The locals say that it hates T.V.

We may never see the likes again.

Remember, you saw it...on CNN.

Beauty and the Beast

I am a hard, unyielding thing!

In worlds of softness I am King!

I burn with lust and mad desire...

No woman can survive such fire!

I lured this Beauty to my cave.

Now it's too late!   She can't be saved!

I do not care how she may feel...

She's but an object of my will!

I ate her up! She is consumed!

All that lingers is cheap perfume!

She's disappeared into my power!

So... who is singing in our shower?

Do I fantasize my wishes?

All right, Dear. I'll do the dishes.

James R. Ivey

Circumcisional Evidence
"I Think He Went to Alabama"

— ❧ —

Dateline, 1990: Nashville, Tennessee.

A lady who looks like a Cuban singer,

And has no ring on her third left finger

Has just made a most unusual plea...

A Minnesota man had been in town...

The local police could not believe her:

"A Golden Gopher has ate your beaver?

The scene was a tent as the sun went down?

Do we have enough proof for conviction?

This whole story sounds so incredible!

Can we prove those things are edible?

I hope that's out of our jurisdiction!

You don't want him punished for this attack?

He's already hung? You just want him back?"

172

Sleeping Beauty
(The Real Story -- Told by the Prince in a Tavern)

She lay like an imitation of death,

With but a whisper of sweet young breath;

I am a Prince. It was my duty

To bring back life to Sleeping Beauty.

I asked her maids to leave us alone,

My magic secrets must not be known;

I kissed her softly, then much harder,

But still there was no sign of ardor.

Then I decided to lift her dress,

And do what I always do the best;

And it was then she came around

And made some most delightful sounds!

Pardon me while I refill my cup...

It was not a kiss that woke her up!

Surprise

I'll leave it all when life is through:

My wife will always have my heart,

To those who love I leave my art,

My son now knows all that I knew.

There won't be much returned to Earth.

My grandchild seems to have my nose,

The Goodwill Store can have my clothes;

I have been giving since my birth.

Death is never our last good-bye.

All those who lived are still alive

In hearts and minds that still survive;

We have not flown through empty sky.

My darling daughters have my eyes,

And Death will get...a big surprise.

True Love

Your beauty boils my ancient blood,

I long to drag you to my cave;

To worship you and be your slave,

Come be my mare. I'll be your stud.

My needs for you are here to stay,

I long to kiss your every part;

To scorch your soul and sing your heart.

I need you more than words can say.

I do not care what's wrong or right.

I need your magic in my nights.

Your woman's cries of pure delight

Have fed my manly appetite.

Now it's over, of course I care.

Put on some clothes, go fix your hair.

Vampire

She was a woman of the world.

This man with whom she was alone,

Was not like any she had known;

He used her like a helpless girl.

She gave her all, but he took more,

He took the essence of her soul;

Against her will she lost control,

And a thing was unseen before.

All dignities acquired from birth,

Were washed away without a trace;

And evil passions took their place,

Forces now unknown on earth…

Later, she found, she was alive…

But what she was…did not survive.

Welcome

Welcome children, into our dream!

Watch where you step!

The earth's alive with things that eat you to survive…

Things are not always what they seem.

Something's waiting behind that wall.

Some say heaven and some say hell…

Maybe McDonald's or Taco Bell…

I'm not too hungry now…at all.

There are some things here to adore.

You'll love the sunshine and the rain,

And your few friends who aren't insane.

Come watch us murder, rape and war.

Welcome children into your dream.

Where things aren't always what they seem.

James R. Ivey

Congratulations on Your Recent Betrothal

Congratulations, dear...

Sometimes just love alone

Is not enough, I guess.

You were very lovely

In your white wedding dress...

The color was all wrong,

But no one knew, but us.

I learned a lot from you.

I know why some people

Always cry at weddings...

And as you drove away

Together, half in love,

In sweet summer sunshine

I walked away alone

Through a bitter Autumn rain,

Daydreams

And shed winter tears from eyes

That shall never see a spring...

Again.

All my new-suit pockets

Are full of unused rice.

I could not bring myself

To throw at you and him.

How long must memories

Live, before they'll die?

In my mind's theater

I retreat to reruns

Of us...of you and me

In older brighter days

When you were my whole world,

And you saw only me...

James R. Ivey

But then diamonds and furs

And mansions and old gold

Turned your greedy green eyes

Away from love...to him.

Now my empty, broken

Heart still holds all of you

That was ever really mine.

I cannot sleep alone

Anymore...you spoiled me

For that you know, I guess.

I have nightmares of you

In sweat-wet loveless sheets

Making payments to him

On your car and your clothes...

Your soul can't read receipts

That lust alone has written.

I called up room service

Daydreams

Just before dawn, because

I was really starving

For you...and dying too,

Of ceaseless hunger pangs.

I ordered up another whore

With bowling ball breasts,

And no real loyalty,

Sunny side up. Ala' Carte.

To go. To come. On demand.

Congratulations.

Lady Mugger

Well, I guess you must be wondering

Why on Earth I am so late;

I was held up by a lady mugger

Packing an awesome pair of .38's.

"Hold up, Big Boy!" She shouted at me.

It's hard for a man to think straight

When his brain can't believe what he sees,

And he's staring at two deadly .38's.

I knew those things could kill a man,

And she never gave me a chance to escape;

To stay alive, a man does what he can

When he's looking down loaded .38's.

Daydreams

She was demanding, heated, and cruel;

I guess I was lucky just to survive.

She made me give her our family jewels,

And left me breathless and barely alive.

A man never knows what he'll do

Until his courage is tested by fate;

My knees turned to jelly it's true

When she pulled out those matching .38's.

I heard thunder, saw lightning, and sparks.

I'm truly sorry I'm late for our date;

A man shouldn't play in the park after dark.

She was a lady mugger with big .38's.

James R. Ivey

A Matter of Breeding

She was already conscious when he knocked.

Normally, she would not have been awake

Quite so early, but today was Thursday,

And Thursdays were very important...

The one exciting day in her dull week

Of church activities and social clubs.

"Come in" she called, as she sat up in bed.

John was, as always, impeccably dressed,

And looked like the bank president he was.

"Good morning, dear! I hope you slept well."

"Yes, thank you, John." She noticed that his eyes

Could find no comfortable place to rest,

And realized her bosom was exposed.

"Please hand me that white dressing gown" she said.

All clothing John 'surprised' her with was white.

She put it on and then he kissed her cheek.

"Umm! I love your new cologne" she told him,

As she slipped on the white satin slippers

That were another of John's many gifts.

Dear John was embarrassed by naked feet.

"Come Dear" he said. "I've breakfast already ready."

"Oh, John!" She said. "You make me feel ashamed.

The cook's day off, at least, I should do that."

Mary gave all house servants Thursday off.

"You? Nonsense! You know I won't permit that.

A kitchen's no place for proper ladies."

'I've heard that" she sighed. "May I ask why not?"

"Why not? Why, it's...just not fitting...that's all!

You were born a lady...not a servant.

I would not have married a servant,

And I shall never make one of my wife!

No mistress in this house's history

Has ever performed a menial's tasks,

And I shall not allow you precedent.

It is a simple matter of good breeding,

And you are the purest of the line.

Now, come! Your coffee is growing colder,

And there are some things we need to discuss."

With tenderness, he gently took her arm.

The breakfast room was on the second floor,

And furnished a view of manicured grounds.

James R. Ivey

James always brought the car around at eight,
But now the only man in view was Biggs.
Peter was trimming the driveway hedges
While summer sun danced on his bare back.
Peter Biggs was a huge muscular black
Who looked quite incongruous among flowers.
"Mary," John was saying. "I don't like it!"
"John, it's only one afternoon a week,
And I really do enjoy helping out...
It makes me feel...useful and important.
You know how understaffed hospitals are...
If you could only see! Little children..."
"It's not the children that cause my concern!
That was not a child that struck you last week!
There's still discoloration in your cheek."
"But I promised to stay out of that ward!
They don't require that volunteers work there.
I was curious then but I'm not now."
"I should certainly hope not, Mary, dear,
But it's not just that...there's bed pans and all...
No! I don't like it and I won't have it!
It is not a proper thing for ladies.

It is simply a matter of breeding!"

"Very well, John" She sighed, "Since you insist."

"I do. You are much too frail and innocent

For such a crude environment as that...

Leave that type of thing to colored women.

You concentrate on your painting and music.

Those are much more proper things for ladies."

"Berserk!" she said, nodding toward Peter.

I believe that it once meant 'bare of shirt'.

"Yes" he said. "I'll speak to him about that!

He will have to learn to keep his clothes on

When there is a white lady around him."

"Yes" she said. "I find that most...offensive!"

"I should release him! His manner is uncouth."

"But" said Mary, "He is a good grounds boy."

"I agree with you there! I had my doubts

At first, when you suggested hiring him,

But he has performed black magic here.

Everything he touches seems to flower.

Perhaps that's because he's close to nature...

He even looks more animal than man."

"Yes" she said. "He looks like a gorilla."

James R. Ivey

James had just brought the limousine around.
"I'll speak to him. I doubt he even knows better.
You know the type: all body and no brains.
Now, I best be going. Have a good day."
"I will" she said as he kissed her forehead.
John was always so gentle with his touch,
He handled her like a porcelain doll.

After John left, she went into that wing,
Where past generations haunted the walls.
John's father, the Senator from Georgia,
And John's grandfather, the Grey General
Who was wise enough to keep his money
In a Philadelphia bank during the War,
And his father, whose slaves built this mansion,
Were surrounded by their most prized possessions...
Even a picture of the soldier's horse.
Among those grand ladies and gentlemen
She had learned the real worth of good breeding.
She felt their frozen aristocratic eyes
That had once made her feel self-conscious.
Smiling now, she removed all her clothing,

And took all the pins from her golden hair.

"Do you disapprove of me?" She asked them.

"Dear John" she said, "Won't look at me like this.

Tell me...am I that hard to look upon?"

She was startled as the door was opened.

"Peter! You nearly scared me to death!

Will you ever learn to knock on a door?"

He stepped furiously into the room.

"You know'd this was Thursday and I'd come here!"

She felt his eyes moving on her body.

"Why did you set your husband down on me, girl!"

His voice told how angry she had made him,

But his eyes told her how excited he was.

This was going to be a real Thursday!

"To make you mad! Will you beat me again?"

"You're nuts! All you fancy whites are crazy!"

"But" he grinned. "You gots a fine set of tits...

Where you want it today, fancy lady?"

He brought an animal odor to her

Much more exciting than any cologne.

She knew that he could never be gentle.

"Right here!" She said. "In front of John's Mother."

189

James R. Ivey

Night Visit

My solitary soul and I sat quiet,
Without a single lamp to light my room;
Outside, no sound was heard, save empty night,
Dark sympathetic silence...like Rose's tomb.

My Rose would not have sat with me like this,
For like a child, she feared the dark of night;
My dear sweet Rose! God knows how dear I miss
The things you were: My life, my love, my light!

When death calls for the aged, men may say,
Such coming is a crowning close to life;
But when he seeks out youth, and steals away,
Flowers as fresh and as frail as my wife...

Such coming is, by all sane minds, despised!
The old lived long lives, and they've had their stay;
But my poor Rose! Death's darkness closed her eyes
In the bright morning of life's shortest day!

190

There is no sane reason in such cruelty,

Fair reason does not room with madness;

There is no logic which can show to me

The justification for my sadness!

When black-hearted Death descends upon youth,

How empty rings God's word and noble creed;

How shallow seems His stream of deepest truth!

Why does he send Death...to harvest His seed?

Farmers who reap the stalk before its prime

Have neither the bread nor money to gain;

When Death cuts down the young before their time;

Is this less madness -- or still more insane?

When Death steals from a mother, life of her child,

And leaves some small nothing making no sound;

A broken vessel...empty and defiled,

Which cannot hold blood, and is cast to the ground...

James R. Ivey

Priests! How then can you ever explain
God's purpose for our lives and universe?
What balms do scriptures hold to ease this pain?
What words from prophets negate Death's curse?

Knowing death lies in her sweet baby's bed,
No wonder a mother is never the same;
After seeing first dirt thrown on the head
Of her child, who died, still calling her name.

How can she ever hope to understand?
No nights of gentle sleep, nor days of sun;
How can the heart you chilled, warm for a man?
Death, you've ended three lives by taking one!

And what of the wife whose young husband dies
In some foolish war, in some foreign land;
Do you wonder that, she often, sits and cries?
Cursing your name -- Death...for all you demand?

'Until Death do us part' is a cruel phrase,
Which should forewarn her of her plight;
But how does she fill empty hours and days,
And how does she face the cold lonely nights?

The love a woman carries for a man
Does not die with bullets that take his life;
Things can never be as they were again,
Until both are dead she remains his wife.

And what of the children he leaves behind,
Who shall protect and teach them to be wise?
Now she must tell them their God is unkind,
Or else must resort to war's wicked lies.

Why do you take from us, our very best?
Why are you so cruel? Why act you insane?
The evil ones...you leave and seem to bless --
Despite longer lives they feel lesser pain.

193

James R. Ivey

You give the wicked time to work their schemes,
Yet cut far short the lives of those we love;
What do you gain by scattering dreams?
Why spare the vulture while killing the dove?

What purpose could your insane madness serve?
It seems that you delight in giving pain,
And seek to see your cruel fame long preserve
In hearts and minds of us that must remain.

Death! I curse your cruel inhuman name.
Death, know that in this room now filled with hate,
Sits one sad man who dares defile your fame,
And damns and dares you...to alter my fate.

Dark knave of night, if you were only here
I'd curse your vile deeds to your ghastly face;
Don't think my light soul would retreat in fear,
You could find a dark foe in this dark place.

Daydreams

There was a day when I valued my time,
There was but one season, and that was spring;
Then with Rose, I found love and joy in rhyme –
Then the birds still remembered how to sing.

My Rose and I were fond of nature's wood,
We were in tune with life -- now thanks to you
Songs of birds and spring have lost all good
They held for me. When Rose died, that died too.

Keats has no truth or beauty in his verse,
The words of Wordsworth are worthless and plain;
Milton is blind...and Shakespeare is worse,
While Coleridge and Poe have gone insane.

Doctor Johnson has no wit, and Frost
Is a simple apple picker -- I see
No romance in Byron -- I am so lost
That even my old friends cannot find me.

James R. Ivey

My own verse that danced on brightest pages,
Lies now unread -- still and dead -- like Rose;
I find no safe solace now in sages,
Their once worthy lines have now decomposed.

That inner voice in me that fired my verse,
That muse who often let my soul roam free,
Thinks art is foolish now, and fires this curse:
Pray Death be damned...through all eternity!

How can a man forget the wife he chose?
Where can he store the love he never gave?
Who shall I duel for defiling my rose
When she lies untouched, dead in her grave?

The well of my tears has long since been drained,
And I wonder who death has marked the most,
My Rose is fading yet I have remained,
To cherish her memory...to worship her ghost.

Daydreams

I live a living Death that knows no peace,
And wish for the courage to erase my name;
I feel eternal pains that will not cease,
And know that all my days shall be the same.

I know that never more shall morning sun
Warm her fair face, or again light my life;
Doomed to darkness, before my day is done,
Doomed to exist without my sun-lit wife.

Who lies buried? The dead or the living?
Does she struggle now, in your cold embrace?
Death! Despicable Death! I am not forgiving...
But would give all...just to speak to your face!

Sitting in darkness makes memories clear,
Of her sweetest smiles and beauty so rare;
I almost feel her perfumed presence here...
Can that be breathing? Does someone sit there?

James R. Ivey

Shall I lose these last remnants of my mind?
I know some strange form in this dark room...
I am mad! Yet, I would rather be blind,
And not see this grave guest that reeks of...tomb!

Whoever sits there has made no remark,
Still someone...or something...is sitting there!
My Rose was bright and afraid of the dark...
The who...or what...now darkens her chair?

"Who are you?" I ask. "Who sits with me?"
Except for strange breathing, my room is quiet.
Is there something there -- or just my fantasy?
Movement! Dark...yet, separate from the night!

"Who are you?   I demand to know your name!"
Silence answers me...cold silence...long unbroken
Silence...pervading silence...quiet as flames...
Burning my soul. "Speak!" No words are spoken.

So, we just sat, intruder and me,
My eyes held fast by the dark silent shape,
That offered few clues to identity.
The eyes were hidden behind hooded cape.

The silence was suffocating! And yet,
I would not flee from that soft silent breath;
I strained my eyes to see the silhouette
Sitting in the shadows...as silent as...Death!

"Friend or fiend...why do you visit this place?
It seems I know your dark and silent shape;
Why sit where the shadows cover your face?
If you are who I think...I won't try to escape.

Really, Sir! You truly are a dunce
To think that I might try to get away;
For well you know, a man dies but once,
And you took my life on Rose's deathday!

James R. Ivey

How could you believe I would want to flee?
Throw off the darkness that serves as your clothes!
Your vile, vain form will not frighten me,
All fears that I had were buried with Rose.

Therefore, Dear Sir...I am pleased that you came.
The sun will soon rise, and then I shall know
If whom I suspect and you are the same...
So, sit quiet and still for an hour or so...

How long have you been with me in this room?
Did you come here in reply to my plea?
Welcome! I would have met you in a tomb...
Shall we now discuss how much you owe me?

'Death be not proud' one holy brother said,
I long to read the pride you may disclose;
Perhaps I may have time before I'm dead...
But now I shall take time to speak to Rose.

Daydreams

Do you recall that dreary day she died?
Of course you do! Lord knows that you were there.
She'd asked me to remain there, by her side...
I said I would...Believing I could bear

More weight of sleepless nights and tortured days...
I failed...it seemed that all my strength was gone;
Now I know she feared you were on your way,
And you might find her, as you did, alone.

If I now lived to be ten thousand years,
This soul of mine could never be the same!
I would cover this earth, with my own tears,
Before I forgot her calling my name.

The time that her voice took to penetrate
My mind, was all the time you would allow;
Did you think your presence could dull my hate?
It was never sharper than it is now!

James R. Ivey

When I recall, she faced that final hour
Reaching out for me, seeking for my hand...
But found yours...the hand that crushed my flower,
And left me with this hate. I understand

That you have no sympathetic weakness,
And go about your tasks without regret...
I understand...But hate you none the less.
Understanding thieves...does not cancel debt.

If it's true that when a mortal gazes
Upon your evil brow, he then must die,
We shall meet once more in Hell's hot blazes,
And there, Dear Sir...I will spit in your eye!

Eastern fire that burns the night to ashes,
Begins to thrust some sparks beneath my door,
And is pushing flames past window sashes...
Soon your face will hide in shadows, nevermore!

Daydreams

Watch close my face, cruel Sir, as I expire,

Pay close attention to my hate-filled eyes,

For there you shall see scorn that may inspire

You on in your vile art a bit more wise.

Look close...and you shall surely know

The extent of hate mortals can carry;

I'll freeze my gaze before I feel your throes,

And pray your memories shall never vary!

James R. Ivey

Noah Gene Smith

Uncle Noah was thought quite odd,

Some said that he conversed with God;

Sometimes, as pretty as you please,

He'd drop right down upon his knees,

And looking up, he'd speak in tongues…

They say he started that quite young.

None suggested he be confined…

While clearly not of soundest mind,

He would rise up, in saintly light,

And make predictions… that proved right!

One day he told our valley town,

A flood was coming… all would drown,

Who did not heed first thunder sound,

And rush themselves to higher ground.

Sure enough, it started to rain,

We left by car and bus and train…

The rich folks fled by plane, of course,

And old Doc left, by scurried horse.

Noah was told by God to stay,

And help his people get away:

"Noah, do all that you can do,

and I will come to rescue you."

So, Noah worked 'till all were gone,

And he was more, or less, alone.

Upon his roof, with saintly glow,

He watched the rising waters flow.

Three boats came by, but he said, "No!"

His God would save him. He said so!

A helicopter was his last chance.

He waved that off too, without a glance,

And waited for God to come down…

The water rose and Noah drowned.

In Heaven, he went straight to the Boss,

And asked that He explain his loss:

"I'm mystified within my head…

My health is good… except I'm dead!

I waited for You to come down…

Why did You stay and let me drown?"

"For one so stubborn, death may be proper…

I sent three boats… and a helicopter!"

James R. Ivey

The Pasture Pond

I'm going to ponder the pasture pond;

I'll only stop, perhaps, to smoke some grass,

(And Crayola the clouds that come to pass):

I do get lonely -- Ya'll come too.

I'm going out to catch that gawky calf

That stands for a second, and then falls down.

Let's push him in the pond, and watch him drown!

That's a nice cloud -- Color it blue.

Love Fairy
(What's This on my Pillow?)

All you boys should be wary...

There's a malicious love fairy,

Who comes out only at night

After you've turned out the lights.

You luck up on a bar room beauty,

A real late-night Southern cutie,

And you put true love inside her head...

And then you put her body inside your bed.

You love her just right, then hold her so tight,

But still you may lose her during the night.

That love fairy comes and steals all her charms,

And leaves someone quite different within your arms.

I never went to bed with an ugly girl,

But I have woke up in another world.

As confusing as it could ever be

I don't know this broad, and she don't know me.

James R. Ivey

A Pocket Full of Rocks
(The Great Ecologist and the Minor Poet)

"But you can't just watch
while the world goes to hell!
Man, you have got to get yourself involved.
Even I can walk across the Mobile Bay!
What can we say to the little children?
Except this world we are leaving to them
Once had fresh air that even men could breathe,
And we're sorry their machines are choking,
While the fish stand around the intersections."

"I have pictured God with a Polaroid.
In this maze where men are measured in pounds,
I am seeking some scale to measure my sounds."

"The hardest colors to explain are blue,
And green, and white, and what was crystal clear.
Throw some rocks in the establishment lake!
When we start to rock the boats they'll listen."

"No. At my bare back, I always can hear
A host of good businessmen drawing near.
Alexander Locke wrote Rape of the Pope,
And Lord Byron swam from Brooklyn to Maine,
While I was filling my pockets with rocks."

"Man, you can't make waves by holding rocks!"

"I can. I'm going to fill my pockets full,
And then jump in and drown the whole damn world.
They'll say: 'Where's all this friggin' water from?'"

"But you must spare America and nature."

"The last American Eagle was found hanging
On a box-kite's tail...suicide was revealed
By a talon scraped note on mountain soot.
The hole they dug to shove the big bird in
Was full of Indian and buffalo bones...
So they threw it in the garbage dump.
Something here is that does not love at all."

James R. Ivey

"Surely saving nature is worth the price!"
"Wordsworth was seen throwing rocks at the birds,
And carving Lucy's name on a tree trunk.
I saw the devil on the six o'clock news."

"But have you no concern for life at all?"

"Life is just a two-act tragic comedy,
With a sad intermission. It's certain
That the hero gets crushed by the curtain,
And no God remembers the role we played.
I learned all the good to know in life
When a two-dollar whore tickled my thigh.
Now the dull memories of garden snakes
Contain all this world remembers of Eden.
A candle is no great comfort in the dark,
When you are afraid to turn on the light."

"Well then, just what would you have men do,
While you are filling your pockets with rocks?"

"You should all gather and go piss in the river."

San Diego, 1961

In this city by placid Western sea,

Where days are clean and white and nights are dark

And dirty, and lit to dimness by green

And red and yellow tight pulsating coils

Of neon snakes -- The religion is love

(Or as close as one ever gets to love),

And every man and woman is priest and prophet.

Blindly seeking sweat reeking, and always

Lost, the lonely men and women stumble

Through swinging doors into black magic

Wilderness in search of some newer thrill

That might restore lost meaning to lost lives.

The night is filled with (if you drink enough)

Beautiful people -- you, you think, are not

Like them, but fate has cast you on their beach

James R. Ivey

And so, you might as well act out a part,

Since everyone assumes that you will play.

Home is so far away that God's own eye

Could never see the things that you do here.

You have the feeling, in San Diego, that

The world ended at the city limits.

You sit stranded on an island where no

Laws of God or man can ever apply.

The night movement has a single purpose:

Get all lonely men and women in bed

Together, off the crowded streets -- decent

Folks must have their rest and precious night's sleep.

Tomorrow they must man arcades and photo parlors

For the ships that launch a thousand faces.

They're disturbed by drunks who cry in the street.

If you must cry, listen to each other...

In some dark eight by ten away from us.

Daydreams

"Dogs and Sailors Keep Off the Grass" their signs

Say. Crying sailors and bitches in heat

Don't stop to read! They heist their legs and rain

On the beautiful artistry of the signs,

And their locked up rutting stains white the grass.

Third St., Broadway, Fourth St., E St., Fifth St.:

Below a million stars gleam one hundred bars.

As day slides into night, the pairing starts.

"Try me! I'm free."

"Sorry...that's too much for me.

I've got the money, sweets, but not the time."

Not the time to love for free...free love holds

On to you even after you're gone...

It's the giving and receiving that ruins

The joy of something for yourself.

From place to place, from bar to bar, lonely

Men go searching for some female softness

James R. Ivey

To bury their souls in -- The night women

Search the faces and forms and try to guess

Which man has the strength to fill their soul.

Honey, life is so hard a cat can't scratch it.

If you are lucky someone will listen.

And if you've been at sea saving money,

You'll be lucky...Money may not buy love,

But in San Diego it can rent it

For as long as you want it (or longer).

The Tropics is my favorite night port.

Vic, the bartender, is a really good friend.

I knew him before down at the Royal.

Nice guy, Vic... sometimes, he loans me money.

With money, you don't have to bargain with

Your soul just to share a night with someone.

Just fifty percent interest. Nice guy.

Beth and her big bowling ball breasts works there.

She'll love me sincerely for Vic's money.

"Not tonight, baby. Give your bare body

And big bowling ball breasts to someone else.

I'll never roll any 300 games with you.

Try your husband tonight -- he's the real sport.

Don't be mad, baby. Maybe tomorrow

I won't feel so -- however I feel...Yea,

Tomorrow I may need you for a while...

To swim in your eyes and drink your soft sighs,

And drown my weary soul in your wetness.

Yea! I may need a gutter for my balls,

But now I don't need you. I need a drink."

Wish I could remember what it was I'm

Drinking to forget...loneliness? Maybe.

The bar girls of San Diego! God's gift

(Or the Devil's) to the lonely Seaman.

Any port in a storm...I feel a storm

James R. Ivey

Coming on...keep your port open to me.

Home! Now so far away you think that it

Never existed except in your dreams.

All the real memories were made right here.

Broadway Carol. God, what she could do to

A man! And tiny Jane, with the perfect

Porcelain body that no one could break.

She had no heart. We were a good pair once;

She liked to see men suffer, and I, more

Sensitive then, made her feel bigger...I

Just loved to spear her small perfection with

My big gaff and watch her gasping fish-like

Flopping to escape the barbed hook that just

Sank deeper and deeper in her softness...

Until the explosion killed both of us.

She made me feel bigger too...I guess

In some strange way, we helped each other out.

And dark-eyed Arlene, the Spanish dancer.

The sun must do something to women's blood.

She screamed and scratched, and the pains of the day

Were not worth the cruel pleasures in the night.

And Ramey, pretty Filipino lover

Of my best friend...he thought that she was his.

Friends should share what they have, but at times

You are wiser if you don't thank them for

Favors they never knew they were giving.

And Sheila...the tallest woman that man

Ever mounted. God, was she ever tall!

She had to have a special bed and I

Helped her break one in... we continued, though,

On the bare floor, and that was special too.

Loving her long-limbed loveliness anywhere,

Was like being devoured by a Boa

Constrictor...I was not quite up to it.

James R. Ivey

"When's the baby due, Sheila? Loan me ten.

Tell him his father was a mean small man.

Tell him his father committed suicide

By drowning himself in a fifth of cheap

Scotch. I'll wrestle you for the ten, Sheila.

Two out of three falls, my love. Surely, you

Can't win again. Be gentle with your holds...

I'm young and I bruise easily...good-bye.

Go back home to Kentucky, where blue grass

Grows. Breed basketball players your own size.

If you go through Alabama, do me

A big favor, will you? See my mother,

And tell her that I'm doing very well...

Good-bye."

Wild West Story

This crazy coot from Colorado,

Claimed he was quite a renegade,

Who specialized in ambuscade,

We doubted his claimed bravado.

Have you ever met a desperado

Who drove a purple Eldorado

And ate peach ice cream on avocado?

James R. Ivey

Witchly Treatment

I was chased by a witch when I was ten,
And I ran until I ran out of breath;
I thought I would not see day-light again,
So sure was I that I'd come to my death.
I hid by the road in a rain-soft ditch,
So afraid moon-light was going to tell;
But she flew right by, that evil old witch,
To keep her date with some lover from hell.
My pride was hurt but I was safe to plot,
Some cruel revenge to assuage my hurt pride;
I vowed this witch would share the shameful lot
That I had known by being forced to hide.
Witches wash those grey wigs, so old folk say,
And they hang them on the live-oaks to air;
Darkness of night sends them off to vile play,
But dawn sends them tracking back to their lair.
The old folk say witches must sleep by day,
So by day I sneaked to the live-oak tree;
I stole her wig and ran laughing away,
Singing: "Bald-headed witches can't scare me!"

Yesterday, Today, and Tomorrow

For Mary, today was slow in coming...
The day light was dying outside and yet
She refused to let go of yesterday...
She wanted to go straight from those sweet hours
Into tomorrow and not know today...
For the first time in ten years John left home
This morning without breakfast—she could not
Look at John and his eggs and his bacon;
Her thoughts were twenty-four hours behind her
And sometimes twenty-four hours in the future.
The T.V. had not been turned on today.
The unfinished novel had been ignored.
She was jealous of her new old memories
And would not have them contaminated
By Viet Nam, Days of Our Lives, or Buck.
She had done only things that left her free
To re-live those precious moments with him...
 She had painted her toe nails harlot red,
And smiled at a woman in her mirror
Who was shamelessly nude and beautiful.

221

James R. Ivey

Yesterday that woman came into existence.
Yesterday, she had blushed like a virgin bride
When she first felt his searching hungry eyes...
But he found some latent spark in her blood
And fanned it to flames of matching desire.
The things that moved her most - his wise hands...
Never before had she felt such pleasure
As his magic burning hands had given her.
Tomorrow, she would feel them once again...
Tomorrow, he was coming here for her.

Later, she rushed in and out of closets
As she had rushed in and out of the bank.
Even while preparing her last dinner
In this cold house that was never her home,
She sat in the theater of her mind...
How foolish she had been ten years ago!
She could have been wise...just practical...
Enough to please her foolish father and John.
Three thousand magic days forever lost...
Ten thousand magic days were yet to come!
This bright thought was enough to make her smile.

And John, she thought: How surprised he will be

When I pull this world down on his shoulders!

Surprisingly, she was eager to see

The shock and hurt and complete confusion

Her news would leave written upon his face...

God! She wondered: how have I stood that man

For all these empty years! I did not know...

His dark infrequent visits left me cold...

I did not know how a woman could burn!

All John can love is money and business.

I'll give him the business tonight! She smiled.

Money? Well, I left enough for a maid

And a fixture to relieve himself in...

That was all I ever was to John.

Thank god, tonight that life will be over!

Great glorious love for the fun of it,

And never to wish I was a man again!

"Mary!" She heard him call as he came in.

It is time, she smiled. Now I can tell him,

And see his stupid senseless face grow white!

"Where are...Oh! There you are! How're you feeling?

James R. Ivey

I worried about you all day, my love…
I say, old girl! Something smells delicious here…
What have we got? Ah, yes! Your good roast lamb."
"John. Sit down, please. I have some news for you."
"What, dear? Oh, news is it? Well, so do I!"
"Please, John. Let me speak. Mine is important."
"Of course, of course! But dear, this news I have
I think you will find much more amusing!
It proves how good you are at judging men!
Remember that fool you almost married?
The chap who wrote verse and dreamed away time?
Thank God, girl, I was there to save you from him!
Your father, bless him, said he'd never be
More than he was then…this proves him right!
He was murdered today! That's right! He's dead.
Some woman I hear he was going to leave…
They say she cut him up into small pieces!
But then, that's no worse than he might deserve…
Remember how he started winching and
Going downhill right after we married?
He just grew weary of acting for you…
I said bad women would be the death of him.

I told you then, he…Mary? Are you well?

Anyway, this is the really good part:

They say she cut off his hands and…private parts…

And mailed them to someone right here in town!

Strangest thing! Said they had a date to keep!

Mary?"

James R. Ivey

Louisiana Lady

She's a Louisiana lady, she's my Cajun baby,

She knows just how to please a man;

She's a Bayou Beauty, a real Cajun cutie,

The wildest little lover in the land.

She can catch a catfish, and cook his head with rice,

She eats crawfish and frog legs, and says it's nice,

She's got a ten-foot gator that sleeps under her bed,

He's a Louisiana yard dog, she just calls him Fred.

She owns a six-foot snake, a real live Cottonmouth,

She raised him from a kitten, he sleeps in the house;

She says kitty is the best house cat in the South,

And we've never been bothered by one single mouse.

She caught me with a liplock on her bestest friend,

And told that poor girl that she was as good as dead;

She told me to watch just how my life could end,

She said, "Get that mouse, Kitty! Sic her, Fred."

She's a Louisiana Lady with dark eyes that glisten,

And when she talks, boy you better know I listen;

She's a Louisiana Lady as I've already mentioned,

And when she speaks, this ol'boy sure pays attention.

Easy boy! Down Fred, Down! What a pretty Kitty!

James R. Ivey

Book 7

Letters...

James R. Ivey

An Unsigned Letter

This is my first real letter to the world.

I have slipped notes in the suggestion box,

But I have not written a real live letter.

I was too self-conscious to sign the notes.

Have I the courage to sign this letter?

Maybe I'll say some something that will help.

Perhaps, because of me, some things may change.

But if I sign it...they will know my name!

God! What will I do when they come for me?

Dear World: I am fine. Sorry about you.

No. I don't really know the world that well.

That rings with too much familiarity.

They come get you if you assume too much.

Maybe I can write more next year. With love,

James R. Ivey

Advice to Young Poets I

To join the masters on the shelf

You must bleed and die yourself;

Don't sit and wait for winds to blow

Get in the boat, and start to row!

No one cares who makes that shore

Our time has come and gone before.

Stand up! Look down! You see the signs?

The minds of men are in decline!

This world won't help us anymore

There is no wisdom to adore.

Do you wonder why God took time

To build your soul with love of rhyme?

Sometimes you catch the air just right,

And then your craft...is pure delight.

Advice to Young Poets II

There are some things a man must know

If he would see his talents grow;

Learn all you can before you start

The active practice of your art.

Before you harvest you must weed

Your mind of all commercial seed.

Plant hybrid thoughts within yourself,

Yours and the masters on the shelf.

In art, you take before you give

Those years you won't have time to live.

Here's one gift that nobody needs:

A man who writes more than he reads!

Order from chaos is your goal,

That is the essence of your soul.

Advice to Young Poets III

For all new things, God gives a season

Was not spoke of rhyme and reason;

Art must be more than fun and games

Golden pictures want silver frames.

God gave us form and laws to follow.

It is ingrained in pigs to wallow;

Do not dwell long on things infernal

When you are kin to things eternal.

Do not risk your soul in friction

All his gifts come with restriction;

Do you think you could be wiser?

You are His Child...not His Advisor.

Sing your songs and never forget

To play your tennis with a net.

Always Spring

If we could live life in reverse

We would avoid some cold mistakes;

People alone are worth heartaches...

Lust for gold is the devil's curse!

I'll leave some letters here on Earth

For my good friends, not yet alive,

Since I'll be gone when you arrive...

Congratulations on your birth!

Life is a rare and precious thing!

Devote your days and nights to love,

The greatest gift our God thought of,

And live a life that's always spring.

Love is yours much longer than gold;

Being warm is better than cold.

James R. Ivey

Imagination
(For Jamie, after Summer Quarter, 1990)

With ten weeks and determination

You worked a year while on vacation;

You showed me what I already knew:

God puts no limits on what men do.

That you did it opened my eyes,

How you did it was the real surprise;

Nothing better can be said of a man

Than "He always does the best he can!"

Tomorrow your best is always better,

Fame waits to hold you if you let her;

Only death has the power to stop

Your rapid rise right to life's top!

What will decide your limitation?

The magic of imagination!

Grandfather Hears the News
(For Alysa, 1991)

If only humans were more caring,

This world might be a perfect place;

We need more honor, love, and grace--

Less of greed and more of sharing.

The 'brightest' of our young today

Say they don't want to bring a child

Into a world that is so wild...

The future comes...who leads the way?

Today, I learned a child will come

The news was such a sweet surprise...

With such parents, it will be wise;

This world will be less cruel and dumb.

"This world is bad! No one can change it!"

Here comes one...who'll rearrange it.

James R. Ivey

To Eden

How would I love you if by chance

We both were free to seek romance?

I'd give you all I have to give,

Every fiber, without resistance.

I want to take you where we lived

Before this world's existence.

I'd love you...body, mind, and soul,

With your sweet essence as my goal.

To paradise, where innocence starts,

To melt this coldness in our hearts.

I want to share one soul with you,

So you would know this love is true.

My love will feel so real and pure,

Without a doubt, you would be sure.

To England

If I shall have one wish before I die,

Then by His love, the gentle grace of God,

I will go home to her, whose sacred sod

Covers those graves wherein my fathers lie.

My broken anchor chain trails back through sea

To English soil, and when I near high tide

I shall go home to fall by Fathers' side,

In Ivy, where they lie in wait for me.

To England, where my roots are found,

I'll take all parts: this sight, this heart, this soul;

I will go home for there I can be whole,

And grow a new tree in old fertile ground.

But if God's grace should prove to be His curse,

I shall send home this single branch...in verse.

James R. Ivey

To a Feminist

I won't pretend to play your game,

I know the difference at a glance;

Regardless of who wears the pants

Men and women are not the same!

Ancient fathers found our mothers

Grubbing for roots outside some caves;

They drug them off to be love-slaves,

A big mistake that lead to others.

The warrior-hunter was no more.

To taste the opium of her breast

He too must grub close to the nest,

And end that life he loved before.

I think that some equality

Is due my brother, now...and me.

To Juanita

I still have that painting you did for me.

Not on the canvas...I think I lost that

In a rent-due San Diego locker.

I keep it now where it can't be lost...

With the other memories of our love.

Sometimes, I sit inside my gallery

Intrigued by the awesome power of your art.

Simply amazed your mind could see so well.

Then translate forces, human and otherwise,

With color, and mood, and force of future.

It's hopeless, and I know now, hopelessly true.

The man is lost within the rings of chaos,

Alone by choice and cataclysmic design.

Thirty years later...the man is older.

James R. Ivey

To Keats

You never saw the 'Autumn' of your life...

A cruel spring wind snuffed out your fevered flame.

You suffered a season of pain and strife,

And you left this field while losing life's game.

You never made your only love your wife...

Still, some art-sons survive and bear your name.

Lord! How much more would our heritage be

If circumstances and fate had been more kind,

And a less frail body had housed your mind?

What wealth would your soul and sight set free

Had your heart survived to seek and to find

Those treasures buried in lost imagery?

Your days were dark, too few, and too frantic...

How can such a poor life be called "Romantic"?

To LeAnna, May 3, 1990
(Who Brings Us Flowers)

Forty years from today, my dear grand-child,

When you're holding a grand-child of your own,

Think of two old friends who wait here alone...

Bring us your flowers...let's talk for a while.

You are so precious! We treasured each smile,

Each hug, each kiss from our Heaven-sent girl!

You brought God's beauty into our world...

Bring us your flowers...let's talk for a while.

Forty years from today, my dear grand-child,

We pray that your life will be equally blessed,

And you hold a grand-child close to your breast...

Bring us your flowers...let's talk for a while.

And when you complete your life's endeavor,

Bring us your flowers...let's talk forever.

243

James R. Ivey

To My Daughter
(For Tracy)

The world is waiting, while you grow,

For some sweet wisdom, free of lies;

That same sweet wisdom in your eyes,

this world of men now needs to know.

Someone decided, long ago,

That toys of death made small boys wise,

But now we find, with feigned surprise,

Wood grows to steel and real blood flows.

But you, thank God, are free to grow,

With lace and love, free of men's lies;

So truth survives in your sweet eyes

For all to see and some to know.

Once in my soul some sweet voice cried...

But I listened to men...until it died!

To Poe

From deepest darkest shadows in your soul,

Moved a phantom file of ghoul and ghost;

Through the hell that was your art, this host

Escaped like floating smoke beyond control.

In your dark moods, you chanted black refrains

Of friends that never knew a woman's womb;

Your nightmare tales and ice-hot songs of tomb,

Have frozen burning visions in our brains.

Blue flames of Hell flash coldly through your verse,

It was that darkest muse who fired each line;

High Priest of Death! Your work became her shrine...

Did she reward your service with her curse?

Today, fresh tales scrawled on Hell's furnace walls

Makes the dead flesh of frightened demons crawl!

James R. Ivey

Plans
(For Jamie – June 1990)

God has great plans for you on Earth,

No child is born outside His Grace;

You are His carpenter from birth,

And meant to build a better place.

Go share His gifts to you today:

Build with His tools of love and light;

Complete His plans in such a way

Your soul delights with coming night!

Not what you had, but what you gave,

Is His measure of your success;

No worth will go inside the grave...

It's left...in human happiness.

So, work for Him and wander far...

God will know...where his children are.

Wedding Day
(To Jamie & Lisset, June 8, 1991)

The Gods blessed both of you at birth

With beauty, brains, and special grace;

They brought you to this time and place

To be bright lights on this dark earth.

What were the chances you would meet?

I think that now you can insist

That love and magic do exist...

And lives need both to be complete.

Today you stand as man and wife,

With hands to hold and hearts adore;

You both are stronger than before...

There's nothing you can't do in life.

Make us some copies of your love...

Children are proofs...to be proud of.

247

James R. Ivey

Graduation
(For Nikki)

Where have your days of childhood gone?

Are you ready to face the world?

I remember when your mother

Gave you to me. Right then I swore:

It will be different for her!

I will catch her before she falls,

And she will never know life's pains;

But now, I see it was the same.

I guess we all just have to learn

The hard way: one step at a time.

Wisdom comes from experience.

I apologize for my failures,

As a father...you were my first,

And I learned, like you, through trials.

Surely now I could do better.

Daydreams

You know, at first your young questions

Were always a bother to me,

For I was too busy it seemed...

And now I know that all my time

Was spent on less important things,

If it was not spent holding you.

Too busy then, now it's too late,

No time to listen, learn, and love.

No memories of magic hours

That would have lasted me forever.

The old have wisdom we don't need.

James R. Ivey

To Theresa

No man alone is ever complete,

He needs a woman to fill his life;

He needs the love of a caring wife

To share his victories and defeats.

I could not have loved another,

Who would have loved me half as well;

Your magic holds me in its spell,

You're twice great as wife and mother.

God made you such a lovely girl,

Now there's some gray in your dark hair;

Still, I'm surprised you think I'd care,

You're still the beauty in my world.

Of all the things that I have done,

Loving you...was the smartest one.

Daydreams

James R. Ivey

ABOUT THE AUTHOR

(c. 1964)

James R. Ivey, Sr. (1942-1992), was an award-winning poet born and raised in Dothan, Alabama. He was a sailor, salesman, scholar of classic English literature, husband and lifelong partner to Theresa, father to Nikki, Tracy, and Jamie (James, Jr.); grandfather to LeAnna, Alysa, Hunter, Dakota and Tristan; and great-grandfather to Kaylee and Rowan.

James R. Ivey (Jr.), MBA, MS, is a Helicopter pilot, writer, speaker, and life coach. He spent 23 years in the U.S. Army and Air Force and is currently pursuing a Master's degree in Counseling. He is the founder of Joy Life Group and co-founder of Ivey Leaf Publishing. He lives in Albuquerque, New Mexico. Jivey1215@yahoo.com